Schweizer Grand Prix Design

Grand Prix suisse de design   Gran Premio svizzero di design

Swiss Grand Award for Design

2023

Schweizer Grand Prix Design 2023

In einer Zeit, in der die Globalisierung alle Bereiche unseres Lebens zu betreffen scheint, muss die Relevanz eines Preises, der sich ausschliesslich an Schweizer Designschaffende richtet, hinterfragt werden. Können wir heute noch die Höhepunkte des Designs feiern und dabei die Farbe des Passes als Kriterium betrachten? Ist die Schweizer Tradition tatsächlich so stark, dass sie 2023 einen «Schweizer Grand Prix Design» rechtfertigen kann? Natürlich haben die Schweizer Kunsthochschulen während langer Zeit Persönlichkeiten aus Design, Grafik und Fotografie ausgebildet, die zu unserem Ansehen im Ausland beigetragen haben. Max Bill, Adrian Frutiger, Jean Widmer, Fritz Haller, Armin Hoffmann oder Robert Frank etwa, die allesamt in den Nachschlagewerken vertreten sind. Und «Helvetica» ist der Name einer Schrift, die es ins Museum geschafft hat und auch Laien ein Begriff ist. Dass im 20. Jahrhundert zahlreiche Designschaffende insbesondere aus der berühmten Kunstgewerbeschule Zürich hervorgegangen sind und am guten Ruf des Schweizer Designs beteiligt waren, ist unbestritten. Wir könnten gar von der «Schweizer Grafik» sprechen wie von der «Französischen Mode» oder dem «Italienischen Film». Aber wie sieht es heute aus? Gibt es tatsächlich noch ein Schweizer Design? Und was bedeutet der Design-Begriff überhaupt, wenn wir damit so unterschiedliche Praktiken bezeichnen wie die Fotografie, die Grafik oder die Mode?

Das Design, das wir hier feiern, ist in unserem Leben überall präsent. Es meint die Objekte, Kleider, Visualisierungen, Texte und Bilder, die uns umgeben. Es kann die Form eines Stuhls, eines Schuhs, eines Plakats, eines Buchs, eines Videospiels, einer Website, eines Bühnenbilds oder einer Fotografie-Arbeit annehmen. Die neue Generation wendet in ihren Erforschungen des Designs zunehmend interdisziplinäre Ansätze und hybride Methoden an: Analoges trifft auf Digitales, Materialien und Traditionen vermischen sich, es wird rezykliert, erneuert, angeeignet, geschaffen und verändert, vom Natürlichen ins Künstliche gewechselt. Die Grenzen verwischen. Die Schweizer Grands Prix Design zeichnen beispielhafte Karrieren aus, ehren Designerinnen und Designer, die die Geschichte ihrer Disziplin geprägt haben, und würdigen Persönlichkeiten, denen ihre verdiente Anerkennung bisher verwehrt blieb. Seit mehr als hundert Jahren lassen Preise und Medaillen Künstlerinnen und Künstler aus allen Sparten in die Geschichte eingehen. Lange waren solche Auszeichnungen den Männern vorbehalten. Auch heute noch bieten die Preise den Kulturschaffenden die Anerkennung durch ihre Kolleginnen und Kollegen. Allerdings kann die Ahnengalerie der grossen Männer nicht weitergeführt werden, ohne dabei die Frauen zu würdigen, die seit jeher zur Entwicklung der Disziplinen beitragen. Mehr denn je ist es unsere Aufgabe, die bisher unbeachteten Namen von Designerinnen hinzuzufügen. Die Auszeichnung des Bundes soll ausserdem dezentralisiert sein und immer wieder auch an Persönlichkeiten vergeben werden, die ausserhalb der klassischen Ballungszentren wirken. Denn die Schweiz verfügt über eine grosse Vielfalt an Regionen, Kulturen und Sprachen.

Was zeigt uns also der Schweizer Grand Prix Design 2023? Mit der Auszeichnung von Etienne Delessert, Eleonore Peduzzi Riva und Chantal Prod'Hom will die Kommission unterstreichen, dass Design ein weites Feld ist, dass es alle Generationen – auch die Kinder – betrifft, dass es eine Materie ist, die gesehen, berührt, gedacht und geträumt werden will, und dass das «Schweizer» Schaffen die Landesgrenzen oft überschreitet. Und schliesslich drückt der Grand Prix 2023 die Notwendigkeit aus, die Designgeschichte unter dem Gesichtspunkt der Geschlechtergerechtigkeit zu überdenken und die Hierarchien zwischen den Disziplinen hinter uns zu lassen.

Nathalie Herschdorfer, Präsidentin der Eidgenössischen Designkommission

Einleitung

Der Schweizer Grand Prix Design ist die höchste Designauszeichnung unseres Landes. Seit 2007 wird er vom Bundesamt für Kultur jährlich an drei Schweizer Designerinnen und Designer oder Designstudios vergeben, die national und international massgeblich zum guten Ruf des Schweizer Designs beitragen. Die Auszeichnung fördert, stärkt und würdigt die Designszene und ihre Traditionen. Die diesjährigen Schweizer Grands Prix Design ehren den Illustrator Etienne Delessert, die Designerin Eleonore Peduzzi Riva und die Kunsthistorikerin Chantal Prod'Hom.

Bei den Vorbereitungen der vorliegenden Publikation wurde uns aufs Neue bewusst, dass eine einzelne Berufsbezeichnung innerhalb der Designdisziplinen zu kurz greift, um die vielen Tätigkeitsfelder der Akteurinnen und Akteure auf einen Punkt zu bringen. Das gilt auch für die drei Persönlichkeiten der diesjährigen Ausgabe, die ihre Kompetenzen und Ressourcen aus transdisziplinären und nicht geradlinigen Karrieren gewonnen haben.

So ist Etienne Delessert *Illustrator* von Kinderbüchern. Er beginnt seine Karriere als *Grafiker* und wird bekannt mit seinen Werbekampagnen und Plakaten. Als *Pressezeichner* wirkt er für die «New York Times» oder «The Atlantic». Er ist auch *Unternehmer* und gründet in seiner Karriere zwei Verlage und ein Filmstudio. Am bekanntesten ist er vielleicht als *Erfinder* des heissgeliebten Yok-Yok unserer Kindheit.

Eleonore Peduzzi Riva ist ausgebildete *Innenarchitektin* und als solche aktiv während des goldenen Zeitalters des italienischen Designs. Sie entwickelt als *Industriedesignerin* Möbel für namhafte Marken wie de Sede oder Zanotta. Als *Produktdesignerin* entwirft sie unter anderem einen ikonischen Aschenbecher für Artemide. In Mailand ist sie hauptsächlich als «*Consulente*» bekannt, in ihrer Rolle als *Beraterin* für zahlreiche Unternehmen.

Chantal Prod'Hom arbeitet nach ihrem Studium der Kunstgeschichte als *Kuratorin* für zeitgenössische Kunst. Schon bald darf sie als *Co-Direktorin* die neugegründete Fondation Asher Edelman in Pully eröffnen. Mit Design in Berührung kommt sie in ihrer Funktion als *Executive Director* der Fabrica in Treviso. Bis 2022 ist sie als erfolgreiche *Museumsdirektorin* für das mudac, Musée de design et d'arts appliqués contemporains, tätig. In dieser Funktion prägt sie als *Vermittlerin* den Schweizer Designdiskurs und ist mit ihren zahlreichen Mandaten in Jurys und Kommissionen eine *Botschafterin* für Schweizer Design.

Für das Bundesamt für Kultur ist die Auszeichnung jedes Jahr eine Möglichkeit, das Bewusstsein für das Schweizer Design und dessen Bedeutung für die kulturelle Identität unseres Landes zu stärken. Ein Preis für ein Lebenswerk inspiriert auch die nächste Generation von Designschaffenden, sich mit Herzblut für ihre Positionen einzusetzen. Für die Ausgezeichneten ist diese offizielle Wertschätzung aus der Heimat und Gemeinschaft eine wichtige Wegmarke: Sie sind damit nun offiziell Teil der Schweizer Designgeschichte.

Die Preisträgerinnen und Preisträger werden von einer Fachjury, der Eidgenössischen Designkommission, vorgeschlagen. Ich danke der Kommission für dieses Bouquet an aussergewöhnlichen Persönlichkeiten. Sie sind der beste Beweis, wie Design unser Leben bereichert.

Anna Niederhäuser
Leitung Designförderung
Bundesamt für Kultur

Grand Prix suisse de design 2023

À l'heure où la globalisation semble toucher tous les aspects de notre vie, il est légitime d'interroger la pertinence d'un prix s'adressant uniquement à des créatrices et créateurs suisses. Peut-on encore aujourd'hui célébrer le meilleur du design en posant une limite telle que la couleur du passeport ? Y a-t-il en Suisse une tradition suffisamment forte pour justifier en 2023 un Grand Prix de design ? Certes, pendant longtemps, les écoles d'arts appliqués ont formé des designers, graphistes et photographes qui ont forgé la réputation de notre pays à l'étranger. Les Max Bill, Adrian Frutiger, Jean Widmer, Fritz Haller, Armin Hofmann ou Robert Frank sont tous cités dans les encyclopédies. Et Helvetica est le nom d'une typographie entrée au musée et connue des non-professionnels. Il est indéniable qu'au 20e siècle, nombre de créateurs sortis notamment de la célèbre Kunstgewerbeschule de Zurich ont participé à la réputation du design suisse. On pourrait même parler d'un graphisme suisse comme on parle d'une haute couture française ou d'un cinéma italien. Mais qu'en est-il aujourd'hui ? Peut-on réellement parler de design suisse ?

Le design que nous célébrons ici est présent partout dans nos vies. Il fait référence aux objets, aux vêtements, aux visuels, aux textes, aux images qui nous entourent. Il peut prendre la forme d'une chaise, d'une chaussure, d'une affiche, d'un livre, d'un jeu vidéo, d'un site Internet, d'une scénographie ou d'un travail photographique. Aujourd'hui, la nouvelle génération menant des recherches en design adopte de plus en plus des approches interdisciplinaires et des méthodologies hybrides, entrecroise l'analogique et le numérique, mêle les matières et les traditions, recycle et innove, s'approprie, crée et transforme, passant du naturel à l'artificiel. Les frontières se brouillent. Le Grand Prix suisse de design célèbre des artistes qui ont mené des carrières particulièrement intéressantes, rend hommage à des professionnels qui ont marqué l'histoire de leur discipline et permet de distinguer des personnes qui n'ont à ce jour pas reçu la reconnaissance attendue. Depuis plus d'un siècle, les prix et les médailles font entrer les artistes – tous domaines confondus – dans l'histoire. Longtemps, ces distinctions étaient réservées aux hommes. En 2023, comme c'était le cas dans le passé, les prix offrent aux artistes la reconnaissance de leurs pairs. Toutefois, le panthéon des grands hommes ne peut plus continuer d'ignorer les femmes, qui contribuent depuis longtemps au développement de leur discipline. Plus que jamais, il est de notre devoir d'y faire entrer les noms de créatrices laissées dans l'ombre. De même, alors que la Suisse est riche de différentes régions, cultures et langues, il est nécessaire que cette distinction fédérale se décentre et valorise également des personnalités qui agissent en dehors des centres urbains classiques.

Que révèle ainsi le Grand Prix suisse de design 2023 ? En distinguant Etienne Delessert, Eleonore Peduzzi Riva et Chantal Prod'Hom, la commission a souhaité démontrer que le champ du design est étendu, qu'il touche toutes les générations, même les enfants, qu'il est une matière à voir, toucher, penser et rêver et que la création « suisse » franchit souvent les frontières de notre pays. Enfin, le Grand Prix 2023 annonce également la nécessité de revoir l'histoire du design sous le prisme du genre et le besoin de faire tomber les hiérarchies entre les disciplines.

Nathalie Herschdorfer, présidente de la Commission fédérale de design

Introduction

Le Grand Prix suisse de design est la plus haute distinction accordée dans le domaine du design dans notre pays. L'Office fédéral de la culture le décerne depuis 2007 à trois designers ou bureaux de design suisses pour leur contribution à la renommée du design suisse sur les plans national et international. Le Grand Prix suisse de design a été conçu comme un moyen d'encourager, de soutenir et d'honorer la scène suisse du design et son riche patrimoine. Cette année, il rend hommage à l'illustrateur Etienne Delessert, à l'historienne de l'art Chantal Prod'Hom et à la conceptrice de produits Eleonore Peduzzi Riva.

Lors de l'élaboration de la présente publication, force a été à nouveau de constater qu'une seule et même dénomination ne saurait embrasser l'ensemble des champs d'activité des différents acteurs de ce domaine. Cela vaut également pour les trois personnalités récompensées cette année, qui ont développé leurs compétences et leurs ressources au cours de carrières transdisciplinaires non linéaires.

Etienne Delessert est *illustrateur* jeunesse. À ses débuts comme *graphiste*, il acquiert une certaine notoriété en tant que créateur de campagnes publicitaires et d'affiches. Il travaille ensuite comme *dessinateur de presse*, notamment pour le « New York Times » et « The Atlantic ». Il est également *entrepreneur*: au cours de sa carrière, il crée deux maisons d'édition et un studio de cinéma. Mais il est surtout connu pour être l'*inventeur* de Yok-Yok, un personnage espiègle qui a bercé l'enfance de certaines générations.

Eleonore Peduzzi Riva est *architecte d'intérieur* diplômée, une compétence qu'elle met en pratique durant l'âge d'or du design italien. Active également comme *designer industrielle*, elle crée du mobilier pour des marques de renom, parmi lesquelles de Sede et Zanotta. En tant que *conceptrice de produit*, elle a notamment développé un cendrier iconique pour Artemide. À Milan, elle est surtout connue pour son activité de « *consulente* », notamment comme *conseillère en image de marque* pour de nombreuses entreprises.

Après des études en histoire de l'art, Chantal Prod'Hom officie comme *commissaire d'exposition* dans le domaine de l'art contemporain. Assez rapidement, elle participe à l'ouverture d'un premier musée à Pully, la Fondation Asher Edelman, où elle occupe la fonction de *co-directrice*. C'est en tant que *directrice générale* de Fabrica, un lieu dédié à la création dans les environs de Trévise, qu'elle entre véritablement en contact avec le design. Jusqu'à fin 2022, elle est *directrice de musée* au mudac. Pendant 20 ans, elle y influence de manière déterminante le discours sur le design en Suisse en tant que *médiatrice*. Membre de nombreux jurys et commissions, elle est une *ambassadrice* du design helvétique.

Pour l'Office fédéral de la culture, les distinctions sont l'occasion de sensibiliser chaque année le public au design suisse et à son importance pour l'identité culturelle de notre pays. Nous espérons que la remise d'un prix récompensant l'œuvre de toute une vie incitera les futures générations de créateurs également à exercer avec ferveur leurs talents. Pour les lauréats, l'octroi de cette récompense officielle par leur pays et leur communauté représente une étape essentielle, puisqu'elle marque leur entrée dans l'histoire du design helvétique.

Les lauréats du Grand prix suisse de design sont désignés par la Commission fédérale de design. Je remercie la commission pour son choix des personnalités extraordinaires récompensées, qui constituent la meilleure preuve que le design est une source d'enrichissement pour notre vie.

Anna Niederhäuser
Responsable des Prix suisses de design
Office fédéral de la culture

[IT → p. 43, EN → p. 45]

Etienne Delessert

Etienne Delessert

Ich schreibe Zeichnungen und male Ideen

von Jacques Poget

Mit seiner scharfsinnigen Formulierung spielt Etienne Delessert nicht etwa mit dem Paradoxen, sondern definiert sein besonderes Talent ganz genau. Schreiben und Zeichnen: Die beiden Handwerke werden meistens strikt getrennt, sogar wenn sie von derselben Person ausgeübt werden, wie etwa bei Dubuffet (dessen schriftstellerisches Talent genau wie jenes von Delessert grosse Beachtung verdient). Sofern sich der Schreibende nicht der reinen Poesie widmet, spricht er im Wesentlichen den Intellekt an. Sofern sie keine rein technische Zeichnerin ist, spricht die bildende Künstlerin vor allem die Emotionen an.

Delessert vereint die beiden Aktivitäten, um «die menschliche Umgebung in Einklang zu bringen» – so lautet jedenfalls die französische Definition des Desgins im Larousse: «harmoniser l'environnement humain». Der Duden zieht auf Deutsch die «formgerechte und funktionale Gestaltgebung» vor. Beide Definitionen passen auf die Arbeiten von Delessert. Auf seine Bücher und Filme für Kinder, auf die Illustrationen von Zeitschriften und die Plakate, die ihn zu einem Meister der Vorstellungswelt gemacht haben, zu einem der «Maîtres de l'imaginaire», wie die Stiftung heisst, die er für den Erhalt von Werken seiner Kolleginnen und Kollegen ins Leben gerufen hat.

Die Vorstellungskraft treibt Delessert während seines ganzen Lebens an: «Die Realität verformen».

Wenn er die Allegorie – oder die Metapher – seines eigenen Lebens in *La Corne de Brume* beschreibt *und* zeichnet, die *Zauberflöte* auf seine ganz persönliche Weise in einen Film umsetzt und aus den Quellen des Künstlers Saul Steinberg, des Psychologen und Logikers Jean Piaget oder des Dichters Maurice Chappaz schöpft, dann verfolgt er ein einziges Ziel: Eine höhere Dimension erschliessen, in der die Freiheit der Gedanken und Gefühle grösser ist. Wenn er das Evian-Wasser anpreist und verkauft, für die *New York Times* die Tragödie des Space-Shuttles Columbia illustriert, Yok-Yok verfilmt oder seine Maus die Welt entdecken lässt, dann erfindet er jedes Mal «die passendste und funktionalste Form» zwischen Konzept und ästhetischen Emotionen. Zwischen dem Marketingprodukt und dem intellektuellen Ansatz oder zwischen der Erzählung für Kinder und den Porträts von herausragenden Persönlichkeiten gibt es für ihn keine Hierarchie: Seine Arbeiten erfordern die gleiche Aufmerksamkeit, die gleiche Kühnheit.

Die Vielfalt seiner sechzigjährigen Karriere vermag zu erstaunen. Nach einem Maturitätsabschluss in Latein und Griechisch entscheidet er sich gegen die universitäre Laufbahn und für das visuelle Vermitteln von Ideen. Er lässt sich in einem Grafikbüro anstellen und erlernt das Zeichnen als Autodidakt. Dabei holt er sich seine Inspiration bei der Zeitschrift *Graphis* und bei den Plakaten der 1960er-Jahre, die von Deutschschweizer Koryphäen wie Herbert Leupin, Celestino Piatti oder Armin Hofmann geprägt sind. Die Sensibilität für die Kunst, die auf der Strasse und in den Zeitungen zu sehen ist, macht ihn zum Erben dieser grossen Vorgänger, wenn auch sehr indirekt.

Zweimal verlässt er Erreichtes, um anderswo Neues zu lernen. In Paris, wo er sich zunächst für seine Werbeplakate die Farbe zu eigen macht, dann in New York, der Stadt von Milton Glaser und der Gruppe um das Push Pin Studio. Er taucht ein, ganz tief: Der Delessert-Stil imitiert niemanden, auch wenn er voller Anspielungen ist, etwa an Bosch (laut Ionesco) oder an seinen Freund André François. Er verleugnet seine Einflüsse nicht und würdigt die Älteren, die Gleichaltrigen und den Nachwuchs mit seiner Grosszügigkeit, aus der die *Maîtres de l'imaginaire* für die Illustration, die Website *ricochet.org* für Zeichnungen für Kinder oder eine Ausstellung als Hommage an Heinz Edelmann entstanden sind.

Aber Delessert wird dann zu Delessert, wenn er auf *sich selbst* hört. Für die Kritikerin Françoise Jaunin gehört er «keiner bestimmten Bewegung an, ausser vielleicht in seinem bildnerischen Schaffen, der dunkleren Seite seines Werks mit expressivem und groteskem Einschlag: Es ist der grosszügige, zeitlose Expressionismus, der allen Künstlerinnen und Künstlern zu eigen ist, die ihr existentielles Unwohlsein in der Kraft der Gestik und im impulsiven Ausbruch der Emotionen ausdrücken. Delessert fügt einiges an fantastischer Düsternis hinzu, wie wir sie insbesondere bei James Ensor kennen.»

Wir sind weit entfernt von einer Schule. Es ist Delessert selbst, der Schule macht im Bereich des Buchs (und später des Films) für Kinder, dies wiederum auf indirekte Weise. Nach Maurice Sendak und Tomi Ungerer, die er als Kollegen respektiert und bewundert, eröffnet Delessert einen neuen Weg. Seine Denkweise erneuert den Bereich vielleicht sogar noch stärker als sein grafischer Ausdruck. Dieser ist allerdings beeindruckend – besonders für die jungen Kunstschaffenden, mit denen er im Atelier Carabosse oder beim Verlag Tournesol arbeitet. Monique Félix, John Howe und viele andere waren dort und haben etwas von Delessert mitgenommen, ohne ihn jedoch zu imitieren.

Ein seltener Fall: Der Künstler, der für sich alleine zeichnet, ist gleichzeitig während vieler Jahre Unternehmer, leitet Teams, führt Ateliers, gründet Verlage und Produktionshäuser, die dutzende von Titeln herausbringen, auch die seiner Schülerinnen und Schüler. «Er hat einer ganzen Generation die Idee und die Zuversicht gegeben, dass das Kinderbuch ein vollwertiges künstlerisches und literarisches Genre ist: Er hat es geadelt», unterstreicht die Expertin Janine Kotwica.

Delessert denkt «als Kind»

Schon seit seiner Ankunft in Paris, als er von innovativen Werbekampagnen lebte, denkt Etienne Delessert an die Kinder und beginnt für sie zu arbeiten. Eines Tages wird er sich bewusst, dass er – wie alle Autorinnen und Autoren – aus den Erinnerungen an sich selbst als Kind schöpft, ohne wirklich zu wissen, wie sein Publikum denkt. Jemand, der mehr darüber weiss, ist der Professor für experimentelle Psychologie und Philosoph Jean Piaget in Genf. Der Waadtländer aus New York besucht ihn, befragt ihn, begeistert ihn und arbeitet schliesslich unter Piagets Betreuung mit dessen Assistentin Odile Mosimann zusammen. Sie führt eine massgeschneiderte Umfrage bei zahlreichen Kindern durch. Das Ziel: Verstehen, wie Kinder auf Geschichten reagieren, die von Erwachsenen erfunden und gezeichnet wurden, und wie sie ihre eigenen Geschichten erarbeiten und aufzeichnen. Das Schlüssel-Album *Comment la souris reçoit une pierre sur la tête et découvre le monde* (eine Metapher für den Geburtsschock) schöpft direkt aus den Ergebnissen dieser Studie, aber auch – und hier liegt das Wesentliche – aus der Fähigkeit des Zuhörens und der Offenheit der Forschenden. Das Vorwort von Piaget ist eines der ganz seltenen Ereignisse, bei denen sich die wissenschaftliche Kompetenz in aller Bescheidenheit in den Dienst eines künstlerischen Vorhabens stellt.

Es geht aber auch um Spirituelles, denn die vertikale Transzendenz durchzieht viele Bilder des Agnostikers Delessert. Selbst die Mineralien- und Pflanzenwelt teilt mit den Kreaturen – den Tieren, Menschen, Monstern und Engeln – zwei besondere Qualitäten: die Unberechenbarkeit und die geheimnisvolle Macht der Blicke. Wenn wir sie betrachten, fühlen wir uns von ihnen beobachtet. Sie sind mächtig.

Überall in seinen Arbeiten ist der Hauch der Freiheit und der Fantasie zu spüren. Eugène Ionesco hat es rasch erkannt und schrieb: «*Delessert entdeckt die Schönheit, eine grossartige Entfaltung der Wesen und Dinge in der Farbe und durch die Farbe.*»

Jacques Poget ist Journalist und Kolumnist. Er arbeitete für die Tagespresse und Zeitschriften sowie für Fernsehen und Radio, war Korrespondent in den Vereinigten Staaten, Chefredaktor von L'Illustré und 24Heures sowie Präsident des Cercle littéraire de Lausanne. Er ist spezialisiert auf Porträts und die Moderation von Literaturveranstaltungen.

Etienne Delessert

J'écris des dessins et je peins des idées

par Jacques Poget

Par cette formule piquante, Etienne Delessert ne joue pas avec un paradoxe mais définit précisément son talent particulier. Écrire et dessiner, ces deux métiers sont d'ordinaire si nettement séparés, même quand l'auteur est unique, tel Dubuffet (dont le talent littéraire mérite grande attention, celui de Delessert aussi). À moins d'être pur poète, l'écrivain s'adresse largement à l'intellect. À moins d'être dessinateur technique, l'artiste visuel s'adresse largement aux émotions.

Or Delessert allie les deux modes d'action pour « harmoniser l'environnement humain » – puisque telle est la fonction du design ; en français selon Larousse, alors que l'allemand selon Duden préfère « formgerechte und funktionale Gestaltgebung »… Les deux définitions s'appliquent à ses œuvres. Aux livres et films pour enfants comme aux illustrations de magazines, et aux affiches qui ont fait de lui un des « Maîtres de l'imaginaire » (la Fondation qu'il a créée pour pérenniser les œuvres de ses pairs).

L'imagination, la grande affaire de toute la vie de Delessert : « transformer la réalité ».

Qu'il écrive ET dessine l'allégorie, ou la métaphore, de son propre destin dans *La Corne de Brume*, conçoive en long métrage une *Flûte enchantée* totalement personnelle, s'abreuve aux sources de l'artiste Saul Steinberg, du psychologue et logicien Jean Piaget ou du poète Maurice Chappaz, son but unique est de donner accès à une dimension supérieure, à une liberté plus grande de la pensée et de l'émotion. Qu'il vante et vende l'eau d'Evian ou qu'il illustre pour le *New York Times* la tragédie de la navette Columbia, qu'il filme Yok-Yok ou propulse sa Souris dans un monde à découvrir, il invente chaque fois, entre concept et émotions esthétique, « la forme la plus adéquate et la plus fonctionnelle ». Produit commercial et démarche intellectuelle, conte pour enfant et portraits de personnages d'exception, pas de hiérarchie de valeurs à ses yeux : toutes ses créations exigent la même intense attention, la même hardiesse.

La riche trajectoire de ses soixante ans de carrière étonne. Bac latin-grec en poche, Delessert écarte la voie universitaire, décide qu'il transmettra visuellement des idées, s'engage dans une agence de graphisme, s'initie au dessin en autodidacte. Il s'inspire de la revue *Graphis* et des affiches de ces années 1960 dominées par des pointures alémaniques, Herbert Leupin, Celestino Piatti, Armin Hofmann, etc. Cette sensibilité à l'art qu'on voit dans la rue et les journaux fait de lui l'héritier, mais très indirect, de ces grands devanciers.

Deux fois, il lâche une situation acquise pour aller apprendre plus loin. À Paris, où il conquiert la couleur, d'abord pour ses affiches publicitaires, puis à New York, ville de Milton Glaser et de la bande du Push Pin Studio. Il s'imprègne, en profondeur : le style Delessert n'imite personne, même s'il est riche d'allusions, de Hieronymus Bosch (selon Eugène Ionesco) à son ami André François. Il ne renie pas ces influences et salue les aînés, les pairs et les cadets avec la générosité qui l'a conduit aux Maîtres de l'imaginaire pour l'illustration, au site ricochet.org pour le dessin pour enfants, ou à monter une exposition-hommage à Heinz Edelmann.

Mais Delessert devient Delessert en écoutant... lui-même. La critique Françoise Jaunin ne le rattache « à un quelconque mouvement, sinon sur le versant pictural, la face sombre de son œuvre : une veine expressive et grotesque, l'expressionnisme large et intemporel de tous les artistes qui expriment leur angoisse existentielle à travers la véhémence du geste et la décharge impulsive des émotions. Delessert y ajoute toute la part de noirceur fantasmagorique que l'on peut retrouver notamment chez James Ensor. »

Nous voilà loin d'une école, et c'est lui qui fait école, de la même manière indirecte, dans le domaine spécifique du livre (puis du film) pour enfants. Après Maurice Sendak et Tomi Ungerer, collègues respectés, admirés, Delessert ouvre une voie originale et c'est peut-être sa manière de penser qui renouvelle le domaine encore davantage que son expression graphique. Bien sûr, celle-ci impressionne – en particulier les jeunes artistes qui travaillent avec lui au studio Carabosse, aux éditions Tournesol. Monique Félix, John Howe, beaucoup d'autres sont passés par là et en gardent quelque chose, mais il n'est pas imité.

Cas rare, l'artiste qui manie le crayon en solitaire a donc été pendant des années meneur d'équipes et entrepreneur, animant des ateliers, lançant des maisons d'édition et de production avec des dizaines de titres à leur actif, publiant aussi ses poulains. « Il a donné à toute une génération l'idée et l'assurance que le livre pour enfants est un genre artistique et littéraire à part entière : des lettres de noblesse », souligne l'experte Janine Kotwica.

Delessert pense « enfant »

Dès son arrivée à Paris, où il vit de pubs innovantes, Etienne Delessert se met à penser aux enfants et à travailler pour eux. Un jour, il se rend compte que, comme tous les auteurs, il crée en croyant se souvenir de l'enfant qu'il fut, mais en réalité sans vraiment connaître le mode de pensée de son public. Un homme en sait beaucoup, le professeur de psychologie expérimentale et philosophe Jean Piaget, à Genève. Le Vaudois de New York va le voir, le questionne, le séduit, travaille sous sa tutelle avec l'assistante de Piaget, Odile Mosimann. Cette dernière mène auprès de dizaines d'enfants une enquête sur mesures. But : comprendre comment les enfants réagissent aux histoires inventées, dessinées par des adultes ; comment les enfants élaborent et dessinent leurs propres histoires. L'album-clef *Comment la souris reçoit une pierre sur la tête et découvre le monde* (métaphore du choc de la naissance) est nourri directement des résultats de cette recherche. Mais aussi – c'est essentiel – de la capacité d'écoute et d'ouverture des chercheurs ; ainsi, la préface de Piaget est un cas rarissime de compétence et d'humilité scientifique au service d'une démarche artistique.

Spirituelle aussi ; car beaucoup de ses images sont traversées par l'axe vertical de la transcendance. L'agnostique Delessert la ressent et la suggère sans jamais l'expliciter. Même la nature, minérale et végétale, partage avec ses créatures – animaux, humains, monstres et anges – deux singulières qualités, l'imprévisibilité et le mystérieux pouvoir du regard : quand nous les regardons, nous nous sentons observés par elles, elles sont puissantes.

Partout dans ses œuvres se fait sentir le souffle de liberté et de l'imagination. Eugène Ionesco l'a très tôt perçu, qui écrivait « ...Delessert découvre la beauté, une sorte d'épanouissement grandiose des êtres et des objets dans la couleur, et par la couleur. »

Journaliste et chroniqueur, Jacques Poget est passé par la presse quotidienne et magazine, la télévision et la radio. Il a été correspondant aux États-Unis, rédacteur en chef de L'Illustré *et de* 24 Heures, *président du Cercle littéraire de Lausanne. Il s'est spécialisé dans les portraits et l'animation de rencontres littéraires.*

[IT → p. 37, EN → p. 38]

A

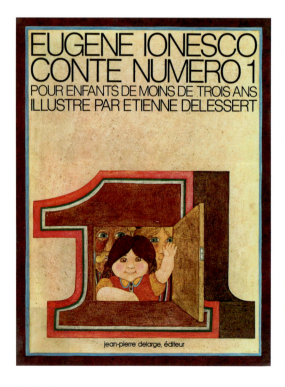
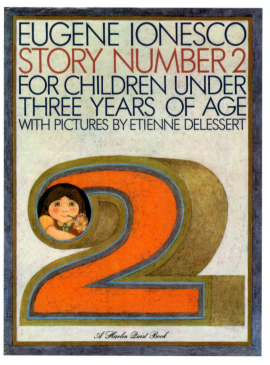

B, C, D

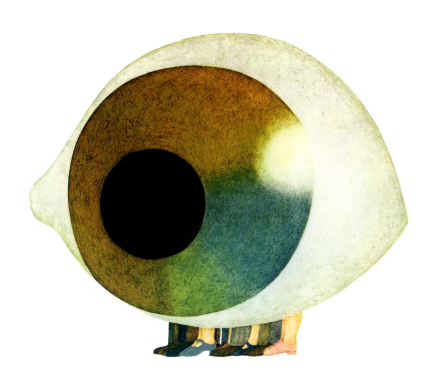

E, F

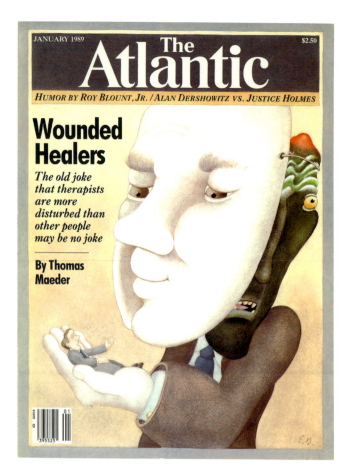
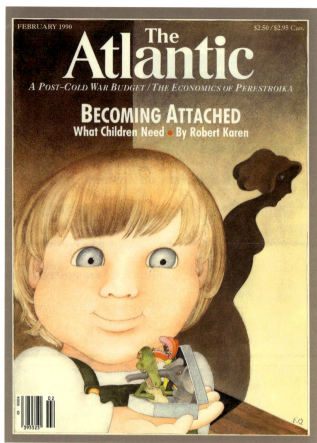
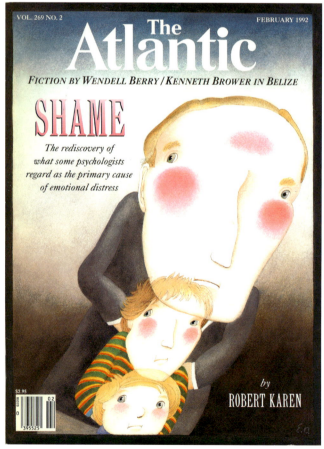
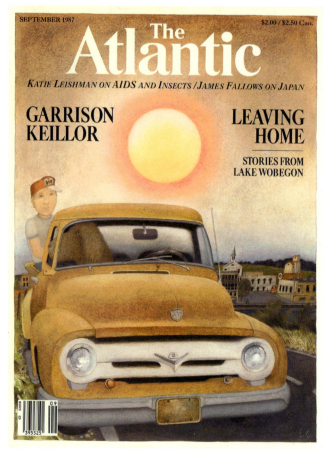

G

H, I

A. *Un ange selon Asimov*, watercolour, 2014
B. Illustration for Eugène Ionesco, *Story Number 2*, watercolour, Harlin Quist, 1970 (*Conte numéro 2*, gouache, Jean-Pierre Delage éditeur, 1970 / *Geschichte Nummer 2*, Getraud Middelhauve Verlag, 1973)
C. Cover illustration for Eugène Ionesco, *Conte numéro 1*, gouache, Jean-Pierre Delarge éditeur, 1970, first published by Harlin Quist, 1968
D. Cover illustration for Eugène Ionesco, *Story Number 2*, gouache, Harlin Quist, 1970
E. Illustration for Eugène Ionesco, *Story Number 1*, gouache, Harlin Quist, 1968 (*Conte numéro 1*, Jean-Pierre Delarge éditeur, 1969 / *Geschichte Nummer 1*, Getraud Middelhauve Verlag, 1969)
F. Illustration for Eugène Ionesco, *Story Number 3*, watercolour, Harlin Quist, 1968 (*Conte numéro 3*, Editions Gallimard Jeunesse, 2008, McSweeney's 2009 / *Geschichte Nummer 1*, Getraud Middelhauve Verlag, 1969)
G. Illustrations for the covers of *The Atlantic*, watercolour, 1985–1998
H. Illustrations for *fact:*, pen and ink, 1966 and 1967
I. Illustration for *New York Times Book Review*, watercolour, 1993
J. Illustration for Etienne Delessert, *A long, long song*, gouache, Farrar Straus & Giroux, 1988 (*Chanson d'hiver*, Gallimard jeunesse, 1988)
K. *Prophets and Pretenders*, acrylic, 1991
L. *Prophets and Pretenders*, oil, 1991
M. *Grand personnage*, oil, 2021
N. Illustration for Etienne Delessert, *La Corne de Brume*, Gallimard Jeunesse, watercolour, 1990 (*Ashes, Ashes*, Stewart Tabori & Chang, 1990)
O. Ella Maillart, illustration for Christophe Gallaz, Etienne Delessert. *Suisse flamboyante. Trente portraits de créateurs*, acrylic, Zoé and Gallimard, 1997
P. Illustration for the animation film *Supersaxo*, ink, 1979–1984
Q. Illustration for Joe Raposo, *Being Green*. A Sesame Street Book, watercolour, Western Publishing Company, 1973
R. Illustration for Alfred Jarry, *Ubu Roi*, acrylic, Gallimard, 2015
S. Illustration for Etienne Delessert, *Jeux d'enfant. A comme alphabet*, watercolour, Gallimard Jeunesse, 2005 (*A Was an Apple Pie*, Creative Editions and Gallimard Jeunesse, 2005)
T. Cover of the deleate Creative Editions catalogue, 1995
U. Play area, France, n.d.

[FR] « ET SI ON REMPLAÇAIT ILLUSTRATEUR PAR ILLUMINATEUR ? »
Entretien entre Jacques Poget et Etienne Delessert, janvier 2023

Jacques Poget: Comment vous sentez-vous, lauréat du Grand Prix suisse de design ?

Etienne Delessert: Le mot « design » m'a surpris ; mais Jean-Luc Godard et Robert Frank ont reçu ce prix, il englobe donc beaucoup plus qu'il n'y paraît. Il est remis à des artistes qui ont le désir de refaire le monde, d'innover, et qui tentent d'améliorer la vie de ceux qui les entourent.

JP: Et c'est votre cas ?

ED: Quand un dessin est vu par cinq ou six millions de lecteurs de la *Book Review* du *New York Times* du dimanche, quand un livre pour enfants est distribué à des dizaines de milliers d'exemplaires, des affiches placardées dans les rues de nos villes, des séquences animées diffusées par la télévision, on espère qu'on va divertir ces millions de personnes, les renseigner, les faire réfléchir, au moins un peu, sur la vie qu'on vit de nos jours. L'ensemble de mes livres a été vendu à plusieurs millions d'exemplaires, je ne sais pas exactement combien.

Mais j'aimerais d'abord remercier l'Office fédéral de la culture pour ce prix, qui m'a étonné car mes relations avec la Suisse officielle ont été… distantes. Ce qui m'a fait plaisir, c'est d'être reconnu à plus de 80 ans, juste au moment où ma femme et moi avons décidé de changer notre testament et d'essayer de faire venir mes œuvres en Suisse (alors qu'aux États-Unis deux musées et une université proposent de les conserver). Donc, merci pour ce Grand Prix.

JP: À 18 ans, vous décidez d'exprimer visuellement des idées. À 82 ans, vous êtes couronné. Cette carrière de 64 ans a-t-elle réalisé votre résolution de jeune homme ?

ED: Absolument ! Par tous les moyens possibles en accord avec le dessin : illustrations de presse, films d'animation, livres. Et bien sûr mes peintures, qui sont plus rudes – souvent très rudes – mais correspondent aussi à mon approche des livres pour enfants, par exemple.

JP: En Europe, le pan « jeunesse » de votre œuvre occulte un peu les autres ; commençons par ces derniers. Vous êtes passé des pubs pour l'eau d'Evian aux grands thèmes des magazines américains, mais n'est-ce pas essentiellement la même approche conceptuelle ?

ED: Quand j'ai vraiment commencé à dessiner, à Paris, pour le Golf de Valcros, l'eau d'Evian ou des produits dérivés de Shell, et pour des commandes du studio publicitaire Hollenstein, je me suis rendu compte que j'avais de l'« imagination dessinée ». C'est-à-dire que j'arrivais à transcrire sur le papier des idées qui me traversaient la tête. J'ai compris que la clef est de concentrer une information complexe en une image forte, proposée avec de l'imagination et destinée à toucher par l'émotion ou l'humour.

Mes toutes premières illustrations publiées datent d'avant mon départ pour Paris : *Kafka contre l'absurde*, pour les Cahiers de la Renaissance vaudoise dirigés par Bertil Galland, dont j'assumais la direction artistique. Des personnages très finement dessinés à la plume, presque un peu abstraits mais bien dans l'esprit de Kafka. Mon approche du dessin est de concevoir des mises en scène

> **« J'ai compris que la clef est de concentrer une information complexe en une image forte, proposée avec de l'imagination et destinée à toucher par l'émotion ou l'humour. »**

de personnages et d'objets très précis, très reconnaissables, alors que l'image qui en naît est portée par l'imaginaire. Il faut toujours qu'on reconnaisse immédiatement ce dont il s'agit – quitte ensuite, au deuxième coup d'œil, à se demander ce que j'ai voulu dire.

JP: Il y a donc une méthode Delessert de mise en œuvre de l'imaginaire pour construire une illustration, cette double notion d'information/concentration qui vous caractérise. Pour les magazines américains, vous étiez davantage qu'un illustrateur : un « commentateur visuel », y compris dans la page *op-ed* du *New York Times*. Racontez cet imaginaire en action. Les rédactions vous envoyaient un article, un dossier… et ensuite ?

ED: Je les lisais, sachant que je devais faire la couverture et six ou huit dessins, demi-pages ou pages entières.

J'ai réfléchi à ma définition de l'imaginaire. Mon éducation classique, grecque et latine, me servait, car les dieux grecs étaient des métaphores, la mythologie est une transposition de sentiments humains et de pensées encore parfaitement valable aujourd'hui. Dans mon fauteuil, je me laissais glisser dans un demi-sommeil et à partir du texte se présentaient spontanément à moi plusieurs solutions – d'idées, pas de dessins. Je disais oui ou non et au final j'arrivais à une idée qui me semblait forte. Je la dessinais au format d'un timbre-poste et l'envoyais au magazine.

JP: Dans votre monographie chez Gallimard, Judy Garlan, directrice artistique du mensuel *The Atlantic*, dit qu'elle recevait vos mini-esquisses comme des pralinés !

ED: Elles étaient minuscules mais expliquaient exactement ce que j'allais faire. On discutait à ce moment-là, et elle se disait stupéfaite, quand elle recevait mes dessins agrandis et définitifs, de voir à quel point tout était déjà dit dans les esquisses.

Chaque artiste est différent. Certains ont de nombreuses bonnes idées et font de multiples

[EN] "WHAT IF WE SUBSTITUTE 'ILLUSTRATOR' WITH 'ILLUMINATOR'?"
Jacques Poget in conversation with Etienne Delessert, January 2023

Jacques Poget: How does it feel to win the Swiss Grand Award for Design?
Etienne Delessert: The "design" part took me by surprise, but Jean-Luc Godard and Robert Frank also won this award, so it's clearly much broader than one might suppose. It's given to artists who set out to reinvent the world, to innovate, and to improve the lives of those around them.
JP: Would you say that applies to you?
ED: When five or six million readers see an illustration on the cover of the *Book Review* of the Sunday edition of the *New York Times*, a children's book sells tens of thousands of copies, posters crop up all over our towns, animations are broadcast on television, one does hope to entertain those millions of people, to inform them and make them think – at least a little – about modern life. I've sold several million books in total. I don't know the actual numbers.

I would first of all like to thank the Federal Office of Culture for this award, which astonished me, given how…distant my relationship with Swiss officialdom has been. I'm delighted to get this recognition in my 80s, just as my wife and I have decided to change our wills and try to ensure that my works find their way to Switzerland despite two museums and one university in the US being keen to keep them. So, thank you for this Grand Award.
JP: You decided to start expressing ideas visually when you were 18 years old. Now, at the age of 82, you are celebrated. Has this 64-year career fulfilled the expectations you had as a young man?
ED: Absolutely! I've dabbled in all forms of graphic art, from press illustrations to animated films

"I understood that the key is to distil complex information down into a strong image infused with imagination that people will connect with emotionally or through humour."

and books – not forgetting my paintings, of course, which are more primal (sometimes strongly so) but also fit in with my approach to children's books, for example.
JP: In Europe, your work for children tends to overshadow your other output, so let's start with the latter. You've gone from advertising Evian mineral water to addressing big issues in US magazines, but isn't the approach basically the same conceptually?
ED: When I really started drawing in Paris for Golf de Valcros, Evian and Shell petrochemical products, as well as doing commission work for the Hollenstein advertising agency, I realised that I had a designer's mind. What I mean by that is that I was good at transferring the ideas going through my head to paper. I understood that the key is to distil complex information down into a strong image infused with imagination that people will connect with emotionally or through humour.

My earliest published illustrations predate my departure for Paris: *Kafka contre l'absurde* for Cahiers de la Renaissance vaudoise, headed by Bertil Galland, of which I was artistic director. The characters were created as very intricate pen drawings, almost a little abstract but very much in the spirit of Kafka. My approach to drawing is to come up with very precise, highly recognisable characters and objects and place them in an imaginative setting. The subject matter must be instantly clear, but a closer look should prompt you to ponder what I'm trying to say.
JP: So there's a Delessert method for harnessing the imagination to construct an illustration, this dual notion of information and concentration that sets you apart. For the US press, you were more than an illustrator: you were a "visual commentator", and that includes the op-ed column in the New York Times. Tell us about your process. The editors would send you an article or a dossier – and then what?
ED: I read it, knowing that I had to produce a cover and six to eight half-page or full-page illustrations.

I thought about how I define imagination. My classical education helped because the Greek gods are metaphors, and mythology is a transposition of human sentiments and thoughts that is as valid today as it ever was. As I sat in my armchair and let myself drift off into a half-sleep, several possibilities would spring spontaneously to mind from the text – ideas at this stage, not images. I would accept some, reject others and end up with what I thought was a strong concept, which I then drew postage stamp-sized and sent to the magazine.
JP: In your monograph published by Gallimard, Judy Garlan, artistic director of the monthly magazine *The Atlantic*, said that getting your mini-sketches was like being given a box of chocolates.
ED: They were tiny, but they showed exactly what I wanted to do. We discussed it at the time, and she told me that she was astonished when she received my definitive, full-format drawings and saw just how much of them was in the sketches.

Every artist is different. Some have several good ideas at once and do multiple sketches before deciding which one to pursue. I always do the sorting in my head, so I only ever need one sketch! My thought process results in one drawing for each idea. I'm blessed with the ability to create a

esquisses avant de choisir. Je fais le tri dans ma tête, et une seule esquisse. Toujours ! Ma réflexion aboutit à un dessin pour chaque idée, j'ai la chance de pouvoir visionner mentalement le dessin final. Bien sûr, je l'embellis de détails, mais le thème principal, je le choisis en amont. C'est la même chose pour un livre.

JP: Un exemple marquant de cette créativité de commentateur visuel ? Est-ce une vision politique, ou simplement évocatrice, sans engagement ?

ED: Cela dépend du texte. Le samedi 1er février 2003, j'ai commenté l'explosion de la navette Columbia non de façon politique mais d'une manière… disons « humaine ». Le *New York Times* m'a demandé une image qui aille au-delà des photos des débris de l'engin. Qui ne choque pas les familles mais montre au pays l'émotion générale. (Ça m'a beaucoup touché que le directeur artistique dise que j'étais l'homme de la situation.) J'ai montré un ange qui tournait autour du globe, comme la navette l'avait fait, et qui perdait ses ailes.

JP: Transposition visuelle d'une information brûlante et de l'émotion qu'elle suscite ; mais vous avez fait hors actualité des dessins intellectuellement violents, par exemple sur le sida. Et celui sur les enfants punis ?

ED: « Punition ou discipline », ma première couverture pour *The Atlantic*, un article signé Bruno Bettelheim. J'avais dessiné un petit garçon au premier plan et derrière lui une énorme main noire/bleue avec des yeux, menaçante. J'ai participé à au moins douze numéros au fil des années et Judy Garlan dit que c'est cette image qu'elle a toujours préférée.

Ces dessins pour les magazines traduisent mon implication dans la vie de la société, ce qui explique que je peux être… violent. Mon dessin sur le sida est provocant, un homme couché dont le pénis en érection donne des branches gigantesques dont les fruits sont des têtes de mort.

Ou bien le motif – un des rares que j'ai modulés plusieurs fois – d'un personnage qui représente la mort et qui tient un archet et joue du violon sur son index. Il montre l'omniprésence de la mort, qui ne m'impressionne pas vraiment. Dans une des chansons de Yok-Yok, le refrain, c'est « Y'a la mort, il y a la vie… » : un cycle de croissance et de disparition. Il y a 23 ans, j'ai failli mourir, empoisonné par un médicament suisse, et je suis resté calme. Je crois au retour à la poussière et ça ne m'impressionne pas vraiment. Peut-être que dans la dernière heure je changerai d'avis, mais je ne crois pas !

JP: Pour revenir à votre métier, comme commentateur américain vous évitez les polémiques personnelles, mais quand vous dessinez pour *Siné Hebdo*, vous vous lâchez avec une verve dévastatrice. Qui est le véritable Delessert ?

ED: C'est quelqu'un qui a vécu en Europe et aux États-Unis, se tient au courant des événements mondiaux, ne s'intéresse pas seulement à la politique mais aussi à ses conséquences, donc à la science, aux problèmes de l'environnement. Et qui – c'est peut-être rare en tant qu'artiste – peut s'exprimer comme on le ferait dans une conversation sérieuse aussi bien sur les relations entre enfants et parents ou entre hommes et femmes que sur les développements dans le pouvoir politique. Ce qui m'intéresse, ce sont une action et un discours sociaux, qui essaient d'aider le monde à souffrir un peu moins. Mais je laisse toujours une ouverture – je ne dicte pas, j'indique !

Cela dit, s'il y avait eu un magazine comme *Siné Hebdo* aux États-Unis, j'aurais sûrement collaboré. J'adorais faire des dessins pour lui, le principe était de donner mon avis, mon reflet de la vie politique américaine. Je réfléchissais à la semaine écoulée et faisais le dessin entre le dimanche et le lundi… j'étais toujours de très bonne humeur !

Je vous glisse un secret : du temps de *Siné Hebdo*, j'ai presque réussi à convaincre un ami financier de créer son pendant aux États-Unis. Un hebdo de combat politique et de dessins, sans lien avec un parti.

JP: Ce travail d'illustrateur était donc important pour vous, pour votre vie intérieure.

ED: Très important ! Pendant des années, j'ai consacré la moitié de mon temps aux dessins pour la presse. J'ai toujours trouvé un grand intérêt à pouvoir commenter les faits et les actions que je comprenais – ou croyais comprendre… il y a tant de choses qu'on ne comprend pas et qui nous indignent.

JP: Cette activité vous a-t-elle amené à vous imposer différemment aux États-Unis qu'en Europe, où vous êtes l'homme des livres pour enfants, Siné Hebdo n'ayant pas duré assez longtemps pour vous imposer en polémiste ?

ED: Je n'ai eu qu'un an et demi pour exprimer des commentaires politiques. Aux États-Unis, je suis connu aussi comme commentateur visuel, mais pas comme polémiste, malgré la virulence de certains dessins, comme ceux dont nous parlions tout à l'heure.

JP: Et en Suisse, cette facette de votre talent n'a jamais été sollicitée.

ED: Si, quelques couvertures et dessins pour *L'Hebdo*, qui a rapidement abandonné sans voir combien des dessins pouvaient intriguer, inspirer, faire réfléchir le lectorat. Je reste étonné que

1. Press drawing published in the *New York Times* the day after the accident of the space shuttle Columbia, 2003

2. Illustration for the cover "Punishment Vs. Discipline", *The Atlantic*, watercolour, 1985

mental picture of the final drawing. I fill in the details, of course, but the main theme is already decided beforehand. It's the same for a book.

JP: Do you have a particular example of your creativity as a visual commentator? Is it a politicised vision or simply an evocative one that makes no judgement?

ED: That depends on the text. On Saturday, 1 February 2003, I commented on the explosion of the space shuttle Columbia in a way that wasn't political but was instead…let's say "human". The *New York Times* asked me for an image that went beyond the photos of the spacecraft's debris, one that wouldn't be shocking for a family audience but would convey the general emotion. Incidentally, I was very touched when the artistic director called me the man of the hour. I drew an angel orbiting the Earth, as the shuttle had done, and losing its wings.

JP: You were transposing a headline news story and the emotion it elicits into visual form, then; but, away from current affairs, you have produced some intellectually hard-hitting drawings, for example on the subjects of AIDS and young offenders.

ED: "Punishment Vs. Discipline" was my first cover for *The Atlantic*, accompanying an article by Bruno Bettelheim. I drew a young boy in the foreground and an enormous, menacing black-and-blue hand with eyes behind him. I've contributed to at least a dozen issues over the years, and Judy Garlan says that has always been her favourite picture of mine.

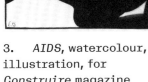

3. *AIDS*, watercolour, illustration, for *Construire* magazine

These magazine illustrations translate my experience of society at large, which explains how I can be…hard-hitting. My AIDS drawing is provocative, showing a man lying down with his erect penis sprouting giant branches, from which skulls hang like fruit.

Then there's the image of a person, representing death, holding a bow in one hand and playing the index finger of the other like a violin – one of the few that I tinkered with on a number of occasions. It shows that death is all around us, and it doesn't really bother me.

In one of Yok-Yok's songs, the chorus goes, "There's death, there's life…": a cycle of growth and decay. I almost died 23 years ago after being poisoned by a Swiss drug, but I remained calm. I think about returning to dust, and it doesn't scare me. Maybe I'll change my mind at the last minute, but I don't think so!

JP: Getting back to your profession, you steer clear of personal polemic when commenting on America but let your feelings show to devastating effect in your illustrations for *Siné Hebdo*. Who is the real Delessert?

ED: He's someone who has lived in Europe and the US, keeps abreast of world events, takes an interest not just in politics itself but also its consequences and thus in science and environmental issues. He's perhaps a rare kind of artist who can express himself as you would in a serious conversation just as well when discussing relationships between children and parents or men and women as when addressing political developments. What interests me is social action and discourse that aim to ease the world's troubles a little. But I always leave scope for debate – I don't dictate, I explain!

That said, if there had been a magazine like *Siné Hebdo* in the US, I would definitely have worked with it. I loved drawing for it. The idea was to express my views on US politics. I'd look back on the week and produce my picture between Sunday and Monday…I was always in a good mood!

I'll let you in on a secret: while I was working for *Siné Hebdo*, I almost convinced a friend who worked in finance to set up something similar in the US, a weekly dose of sharp, non-partisan political commentary with illustrations.

JP: Your work as an illustrator was important to you psychologically, then.

ED: Very much so! For years, I devoted half my time to press illustrations. I was always very interested in being able to comment on the facts and events I understood – or believed I understood…there are so many things that we don't understand and get worked up about.

4. *Dance of Death*, Acrylograph, 1976

JP: Did you find this work different in the US compared with Europe, where you are known for children's books, given that *Siné Hebdo* was not around long enough for you to establish yourself as a polemicist?

ED: I only had a year and a half to practise political commentary. In the US, I'm also known as a visual commentator, but not as a polemicist, despite the mordancy of some of my drawings, like those we just discussed.

JP: In Switzerland, on the other hand, no one ever called on this aspect of your talent.

ED: Some did, actually. There were a few covers and some illustrations for *L'Hebdo*, which quickly threw in the towel before it could see how powerful illustrations could be in terms of drawing readers in, inspiring them, making them think. To this day, I'm still astounded that Switzerland, which had an excellent reputation in the graphic arts at that time, never considered running thought-provoking illustrations in its press that appeal to the intellect rather than just humorous cartoons.

Few were interested in the intellectual and emotional power of a drawing. I found this out for

la Suisse, qui jouissait à l'époque d'une grande renommée pour ses arts graphiques, ait ignoré la notion même de s'adresser au public dans la presse écrite par des dessins spirituels ; au sens non d'amusant mais de « parlant à l'esprit », plein de réflexion.

L'apport intellectuel et d'émotion d'un dessin n'intéressait pas grand monde, je l'ai vécu lorsqu'une grande galeriste lausannoise désireuse de m'exposer m'a dit : « Nous allons travailler ensemble des années et des années, mais il va falloir que vous abandonniez les livres et les affiches. » Exclu ! C'eût été abandonner l'idée même qui m'avait inspiré à 21 ans : m'adresser non pas, progressivement, au public de galeries de plus en plus importantes, mais directement à des millions de personnes qui ouvrent leur journal le matin et marchent dans la rue.

Ce qui a été le cas ici, aux États-Unis, où je suis simultanément l'homme des livres pour enfants : beaucoup ont été publiés d'abord par des éditeurs américains !

JP: Pourtant, votre intérêt pour ce genre est né plus tôt, à Paris, après votre formation lausannoise de graphiste. Comment le livre pour enfants a-t-il conquis votre vie ?

ED: Tout graphiste qui dessine a envie de faire un livre pour enfants. De raconter une histoire. Un film, c'est très cher, il est plus simple de faire un livre, et je pouvais m'exprimer pleinement par ce moyen. Et autre chose aussi : j'ai toujours aimé m'exprimer de façons fort diverses.

JP: Pourquoi pas alors de la bande dessinée, tout public ?

ED: Je n'ai pas eu envie de faire de la BD : toute mon éducation graphique était de concentrer les informations en une image, pas de raconter comment un personnage entre et sort d'une chambre – je force le trait mais c'est vrai. Concentrer l'imaginaire ! Peut-être aussi qu'entre dans mon goût pour le livre pour enfants un héritage de l'enfance : le souvenir des albums du Père Castor (*Michka !*) ou d'Alois Carigiet.

Et puis, tout simplement, j'ai eu une enfance heureuse et, comme Maurice Sendak ou Jean-Claude Carrière, j'ai trouvé qu'« un enfant vaut parfois davantage qu'un adulte ». C'est-à-dire que je m'adresse à un public perméable, avide d'apprendre, qui découvre le monde et espère l'améliorer. On peut l'emmener dans des chemins magiques, il accepte de parler à un caillou ; pour lui, un oiseau ou un renard, une souris, ne sont pas des êtres étrangers mais font partie inhérente de son monde.

Contrairement à trop de livres qui ne font que décrire des situations de tous les jours sans y mettre la moindre parcelle d'imagination ou de magie, dans les années 1960-1970 quelques artistes

« Qu'est-ce que l'imaginaire ? Transformer la réalité, lui donner une forme et, dans le cas de livres, lui donner une forme par une histoire. »

européens et américains proposaient aux enfants des mondes imaginés, qui élargissaient la vision ; décrire de façon réaliste des scènes de la vie quotidienne, avec de l'humour de cour d'école, ça ne m'intéresse guère.

JP: Imaginaire est votre maître-mot, vous avez créé la fondation Les Maîtres de l'imaginaire… Que mettez-vous dans ce terme ?

ED: L'essentiel ! Qu'est-ce que l'imaginaire ? Transformer la réalité, lui donner une forme et, dans le cas de livres, lui donner une forme par une histoire.

J'ai eu de la chance, celles et ceux qui aiment mes livres ont compris dès mes débuts qu'ils peuvent être lus à des enfants et partagés avec leurs parents. Mes dessins ne sont pas simplifiés « pour mieux parler aux enfants ». Ils sont mis en scène, amplement dessinés, formellement achevés. Comme mes devanciers ou collègues, tous amis, Maurice Sendak, Tomi Ungerer, Domenico Gnoli, Alain Le Foll, André François, Heinz Edelmann, j'ai compris très tôt que, d'une manière souvent naïve mais subtile, les enfants vivent les mêmes émotions positives et négatives que les adultes. Avec une grande différence, qu'il faut souligner à nouveau : ils ont encore l'espoir de pouvoir changer les choses, la vie de ceux qui les entourent pour qu'ils vivent plus harmonieusement.

JP: Vous saviez cela, mais vous avez quand même demandé à un grand savant de vous aider à mieux comprendre les enfants…

ED: J'avais publié plusieurs livres avant d'aller consulter Jean Piaget à Genève. Avec ma compagne Eléonore Schmid, nous étions partis de Paris pour les États-Unis, où nous avons créé nos premiers livres pour enfants, deux cosignés, puis chacun à notre nom tout en travaillant ensemble. Des livres remarqués…

JP: Révolutionnaires.

ED: Un grand mot, disons novateurs. Mais, un jour, j'ai voulu savoir si les enfants réagissaient vraiment comme je le croyais en me fiant à mes propres souvenirs. Jean Piaget a accepté de confier à son assistante Odile Mosimann un programme de recherche auprès d'enfants de cinq à six ans (aujourd'hui, ce serait plutôt trois ou quatre ans…) sur leur réception des histoires imaginées par les adultes, et sur les histoires qu'eux-mêmes imaginent. Et j'ai publié *Comment la souris reçoit une pierre sur la tête et découvre le monde*.

JP: Odile Mosimann a-t-elle tiré de cette enquête un article scientifique ?

ED: Je ne crois pas, elle a laissé Piaget utiliser ce matériel pour la préface. Parce qu'à la fin de ce travail de huit mois, je lui ai montré les dessins et le texte finis, et il m'a timidement demandé s'il pouvait préfacer le livre.

JP: Cette préface est donc la seule chose qui reste de ce travail scientifique.

myself when a leading gallery owner in Lausanne who wanted to exhibit my work said to me, "We're going to work together for many years, but you'll have to ditch the books and posters." No chance! That would mean turning my back on the very idea that inspired me at the age of 21: not striving to appeal to the sort of people who go to galleries, which were steadily gaining importance, but instead directly addressing the millions of people who open up a newspaper every morning as they walk down the street.

That's what I did here, in the US, although I'm known for children's books here too. Many of them were first published by American companies, you know!

JP: Nevertheless, your interest in this genre was awakened earlier, in Paris, after you trained as a graphic designer in Lausanne. How did children's books take over your life?

ED: Anyone who draws professionally wants to work on a book for children, to tell a story. Films are very expensive to make, books are much simpler, and I was able to express myself fully in this medium. And another thing: I've always enjoyed expressing myself in a wide range of different ways.

JP: So why did you never produce a comic book with a broader appeal?

ED: I never wanted to do a comic book. My entire training in graphic design was about condensing information into an image, not showing a character entering and leaving a room. I'm exaggerating, but there's some truth in that. Condensing the imaginary! My affinity for children's books might well stem from my own childhood, from my memories of albums by Père Castor (like *Michka*) and Aloïs Carigiet.

Put simply, I had a happy childhood, and – like Maurice Sendak and Jean-Claude Carrière – I found that "a child is…often even more than an adult". In other words, I have a receptive audience

"What is imagination? It's about transforming reality, giving it a form and, in the case of books, doing so through a story."

that is keen to learn, that is discovering the world and wants to make it better. Children can be taken on magical journeys, they don't think twice about chatting to a pebble. Birds, foxes, mice are not strange creatures to them but integral parts of their world.

Unlike too many books that just describe everyday situations without an ounce of imagination or magic, some European and American artists in the 1960s and 1970s offered children imaginary worlds that broadened their minds. Realistic descriptions of scenes from ordinary life coloured with playground humour aren't really of interest to me.

JP: The imaginary is paramount for you, and you set up the foundation Les Maîtres de l'Imaginaire… what does the term mean to you?

ED: It's the be all and end all! What is imagination? It's about transforming reality, giving it a form and, in the case of books, doing so through a story.
I've been lucky in that those who love my books understood right from the start that they could be read to children and shared with their parents. My illustrations aren't simplified for children, they're carefully composed, detailed and fully formed. Like my predecessors and my contemporaries Maurice Sendak, Tomi Ungerer, Domenico Gnoli, Alain Le Foll, André François and Heinz Edelmann (all friends of mine), I understood very early on that children experience the same emotions, both positive and negative, as adults, albeit often in a naïve, subtle way. The big difference, I must reiterate, is that they still have hope in their ability to change things, to change the lives of those around them for the better.

JP: You already knew that, but you asked a great scientist to help you understand children better…

ED: I'd put out several books before I went to consult Jean Piaget in Geneva. Accompanied by Eléonore Schmid, I set out from Paris to the US, where we created our first books for children: two under both our names, then continuing to work together but on separate works under our own names. They were well received…

JP: Revolutionary, even.

ED: That's a big word. Let's say "innovative". At any rate, I felt the need to find out whether children really did respond how I thought based on my own memories of childhood. Jean Piaget agreed to second his assistant Odile Mosimann to a research programme involving children aged five to six (it would probably be three or four today…), looking at how they react to stories thought up by adults and the stories they think up for themselves. That's when I wrote *How the mouse was hit on the head by a stone and so discovered the world*.

JP: Did Odile Mosimann write a scientific paper based on this research?

ED: I don't think so, she let Piaget use her material for the foreword. At the end of eight months of work, I showed him the finished drawings and text, and he timidly asked if I would let him write a foreword for the book.

JP: So that foreword is all that remains of the research?

ED: At the time, it really worried French-speaking publishers and artists, who began to wonder if they would have to test all their manuscripts on children. I pointed out that the book was experimental, and, enriched by the experience, I continued to produce books that had nothing to do with school experiments. I always kept the ambition to create stories that were also metaphors or parables, albeit not explicitly. I wanted to leave room for children's imagination – and that of their parents!

ED: À l'époque, elle avait beaucoup troublé les éditeurs français et les artistes, ils se demandaient s'ils allaient devoir soumettre systématiquement leurs manuscrits à des enfants ! Je répétais pourtant que ce livre était expérimental, et je continuais, enrichi par cette expérience, à faire des livres qui n'avaient rien à voir avec des expériences dans des écoles. J'ai toujours conservé l'ambition de créer des histoires qui soient aussi des métaphores ou des paraboles pas directement explicites. De laisser de la place à l'imaginaire des enfants. Et de leurs parents !

JP: Il faut dire que certaines de vos créatures sont inquiétantes. Correspondent-elles à une idée que vous voulez faire passer aux enfants ou est-ce votre imaginaire, sans filtre ?

ED: Imaginaire sans filtre ! Mais à propos de Piaget : ce n'était pas un psychologue-phénoménologue qui étudiait les enfants pour eux-mêmes, il voulait mieux comprendre les adultes en étudiant les enfants. Il essayait de savoir à travers les âges ce qu'il y avait de permanent. Et je me situe assez près de cette démarche. Ce sont les gens, leurs actions, leurs pensées qui m'intéressent.

JP: Ce qui vous a conduit à expérimenter tous azimuts, y compris le cinéma d'animation. Notamment à imaginer le personnage de Yok-Yok, décliné ensuite en livres, alors que d'habitude c'est l'inverse.

ED: J'avais un studio, avec des collaborateurs, nous faisions des films courts – une à quatre minutes pour *Sesame Street*, treize pour ma *Souris*. La société qui s'occupait de la publicité à la TV suisse m'a commandé 150 films de 10 secondes pour séparer, le soir, le bloc de pub et les émissions. Avec mon épouse d'alors, Anne van der Essen, nous avons conçu deux séquences sur la nature, avec des grenouilles et un pic épeiche, sans personnage humain. Les commanditaires aimaient beaucoup mais voulaient un personnage, présent dans chaque épisode. J'étais navré, car pour moi un « personnage » risquait d'être caricatural. J'allais abandonner, mais j'ai fait un croquis… le chapeau est devenu de plus en plus grand, le visage était simplement un visage d'enfant comme je les dessinais. Yok-Yok est né comme ça et la série a commencé. Elle m'a permis – mon esprit d'entrepreneur ! – de développer l'équipe du studio Carabosse, nous sommes passés à trente ou cinquante et avons réalisé des films publicitaires et médicaux.

5. Jean Piaget, illustration for *Redbook* magazine, gouache, 1972

JP: Et lancé le projet *Supersaxo*, long métrage d'animation finalement échoué sur les écueils financiers. Il était basé sur vos illustrations pour le livre *Le Match Valais-Judée* de Maurice Chappaz dont s'inspirait le scénario. Aventure épique et désespérante …

ED: … dont il ne reste que des planches, des éléments de décor et tout de même 23 minutes de film !

JP: J'ai gardé pour la fin la question qu'on ne pose pas à un artiste : quelles sont les particularités de votre art ?

ED: La couleur tient un grand rôle, et je joue avec des techniques adaptées à chaque sujet. Je vous ai dit que mes dessins sont formellement achevés, mes aquarelles frottées sont une manière très juste de rendre des brumes, des personnages, des couleurs, et de mettre en valeur des mises en scène.

JP: Aquarelles frottées ?

ED: Je frotte, oui, j'égalise. Avec un mouchoir en tissu et un tout petit peu d'eau… ou bien un peu de salive (mon ADN est sur beaucoup de mes œuvres !). Ça me permet d'effacer les touches du pinceau et de dégrader. Je le fais avec l'aquarelle, mais j'ai commencé jadis avec la gouache, diluée. Je voulais obtenir une matière qui soit quasiment la même que celle de l'aquarelle, et je posais

« J'ai toujours conservé l'ambition de créer des histoires qui soient aussi des métaphores ou des paraboles pas directement explicites. De laisser de la place à l'imaginaire des enfants. Et de leurs parents ! »

la couleur pour un ciel en le dégradant déjà mais en laissant un peu visibles les coups de pinceaux. Maintenant, en frottant, j'égalise la couleur pour rejoindre le blanc du papier. Quand on arrive au bas d'un ciel dégradé ou à la face pâle d'un personnage, je frotte pour passer avec une grande douceur de la couleur au blanc.

Et je termine toujours avec des crayons – des Prismacolor américains – assez gras pour avoir une belle couleur quand on appuie mais assez durs pour être taillés très fins.

Souvent, j'ai choisi l'acrylique pour réaliser mes portraits, par exemple la série *Suisse flamboyante*, avec la même finesse technique. L'acteur Michel Simon, l'écrivain Blaise Cendrars ont un visage sculpté, modelé, de la même manière que je dessine à l'aquarelle pour mes livres. Il y a donc une correspondance entre ma vision de la technique et de la forme. Certains de mes portraits de chats n'en sont plus vraiment, ce sont plutôt des peintures sur l'idée féline. Et dans quelques-uns de mes *Prophètes et charlatans*, il y a une liberté de geste et un évident plaisir de peindre.

JP: Mais vous parliez de « mise en scène »…

ED: Elle est absolument essentielle. Comme au théâtre ou au cinéma, les éléments sont clairement présentés, les personnages et les situations saisis au premier coup d'œil. Et dès qu'on essaie de comprendre l'ensemble de la scène, puis de l'histoire, alors on en perçoit la profondeur. Je veux permettre des interprétations par le lecteur.

JP: It must be said that some of your creatures are disturbing. Do these correspond to ideas you wanted to convey to children, or are they the product of your unfiltered imagination?

ED: Unfiltered imagination! Getting back to Piaget, he wasn't a psychologist-phenomenologist studying children in their own right, he studied them in order to gain a better understanding of adults. He sought constants that do not change with age, and my approach is not too far removed from this. I'm interested in people, how they act and how they think.

JP: This led you to experiment with all sorts of media, including animation. Your most notable creation here was Yok-Yok, who subsequently appeared in books. It usually happens the other way round.

6. Illustration for Etienne Delessert, *Jeux d'enfant. A comme alphabet*, watercolour, Gallimard Jeunesse, 2005 (*A Was an Apple Pie*, Creative Editions and Gallimard Jeunesse, 2005)

ED: I had a studio with some staff, and we made short films – one to four minutes long for Sesame Street, 13 minutes for my *Mouse*. The company in charge of advertising on Swiss TV commissioned 150 ten-second films from me to slot between commercial breaks and programmes in the evenings. Together with my wife at the time, Anne van der Essen, I thought up two sequences on the theme of nature, some frogs and a woodpecker, not anthropomorphised. The client was very impressed but wanted a character to appear in each episode. This upset me because I thought a "character" would risk becoming a caricature. I was all set to give up, but then I made a rough sketch…the hat got bigger and bigger, the face was simply a child's face the way I normally drew it. Yok-Yok was born, and the series began. I'm something of an entrepreneur, so this made it possible to expand the staff of the Carabosse studio from 30 to 50, and we produced commercials and medical films.

JP: You also began the *Supersaxo* project, a feature-length animated film that was ultimately undone by funding problems. It was based on your illustrations for the Maurice Chappaz book *Le match Valais-Judée* that inspired the plot. A heartbreaking, epic adventure…

ED: …of which all that remains are a few plates, pieces of scenery and some 23 minutes of footage!

JP: I have saved the question one should not ask an artist for last: what makes your art unique?

ED: Colour plays a big role, and I play with techniques, adapting them to each subject. As I said earlier, my drawings are fully formed, while my rubbed watercolours are a great way of creating misty scenes, breathing life into characters and scenes and adding colour.

JP: Rubbed watercolours?

"I always kept the ambition to create stories that were also metaphors or parables, albeit not explicitly. I wanted to leave room for children's imagination – and that of their parents!"

ED: Yes, I rub the paint to spread it around. I use a cloth and a little water…or even spit (my DNA is on a lot of my works). It lets me blur out the brush strokes and smudge the paint. I do it with watercolours, but I used to use diluted gouache. I wanted a medium that was almost the same as watercolour, and I would smudge the colour for a sky, just leaving faint traces of brushstrokes visible. These days, I rub the colour in to blend it with the white of the paper. When I get to the base of a smudged sky or the pale face of a character, I use rubbing to create a very soft transition between colour and white.

I always finish with pencils – Prismacolor from the US, oily enough to put down some nice colour and yet hard enough to be sharpened very finely.

I would often choose acrylics for my portraits, like the series *La Suisse flamboyante*, with the same technical finesse. The portraits of the actor Michel Simon or the writer Cendrars have sculpted, modelled faces, the same way that I use watercolours for my books. There's a link, then, between my visions of technique and form. Some of my portraits of cats aren't really portraits at all, they are more like paintings of the feline essence. One or two of my *Prophets and Pretenders* display a freedom of gesture and an obvious joy of painting.

JP: You mentioned "scenes"…

ED: They're absolutely essential. Just like in theatre or cinema, the elements are clearly presented, the characters and situations are immediately apparent. When you try to understand the scene as a whole, then the story, you see the depth. I want to give the reader scope for interpretation.

7. Illustration for Etienne Delessert, *La Corne de brume*, watercolour, Gallimard jeunesse, 1990 (*Ashes, Ashes*, Stewart, Tabori & Chang, 1990)

Let's take a complicated piece like Ionesco's *Stories* as an example. The characters are well defined, their interactions obvious, but the general meaning of the scene is ambiguous, it's up to the reader to engage with it.

JP: Can you cite another example?

ED: Yes, something very simple: a group of characters dressed in red, slicing apples to make a tart, with one of them getting a face full of flour.

At first, we see that they are working together, but then we start to wonder how well. With their other-worldly faces, they are genuine characters, and we might ask what's really going on in this scene that appears unambiguous at first glance.

The same is true of *Ashes, Ashes*, which I consider to be one of my best books. You could see it as

Prenons un dessin compliqué, par exemple pour les *Contes* de Ionesco. Les personnages sont bien définis, leur interaction évidente, mais la signification générale de la scène est ambigüe, et c'est au lecteur de s'y engager.

JP: Un autre exemple ?

ED: Une chose toute simple, ces personnages habillés en rouge qui coupent des pommes pour en faire une tarte, et balancent de la farine au visage de l'un d'entre eux.

D'abord on voit bien qu'ils collaborent, ensuite on se dit « mais s'entendent-ils vraiment ? ». Avec leurs têtes venues d'un autre monde, ce sont de vrais personnages, et on peut se demander ce qui se joue véritablement dans cette scène qui au premier abord semble univoque.

C'est aussi le cas dans *La corne de brume*, à mes yeux un de mes meilleurs livres. À certains égards une métaphore de mes changements de continents. Un album écrit et dessiné, en solitaire. Il serait trop long de raconter cette histoire d'émigration, à la fois parfaitement compréhensible pour des enfants de quatre à huit ans et pleine de sous-entendus qui parleront aux adultes. Avec Jean-Claude Carrière, nous avons travaillé sur un scénario pour en faire un long-métrage.

JP: L'entretien s'achève, beaucoup de grands absents …

ED: … trop nombreux même pour ne citer que leurs noms. Alors au moins Rita Marshall, mon épouse depuis 40 ans. Une formidable typographe – en fait, une directrice artistique, elle travaille avec les artistes et les écrivains dès la première ligne et la première esquisse. Quand on fera l'éloge de ce qu'elle a réalisé pendant 30 ans avec Creative Editions, on se rendra compte qu'elle est une designer complète, au sens où elle a mis en valeur l'œuvre de multiples créateurs : il y a quelque chose d'elle dans chacun de ces livres. Nous avons travaillé côte à côte, mais aussi ensemble pour plusieurs livres. Elle en a écrit deux : *I Hate To Read!* (*J'aime pas lire !*) et *I Still Hate To Read!* (*J'aime vraiment pas lire !*).

JP: Un dernier mot ?

ED: Dans ce qui nous entoure, il faut voir le bien et le mal, la méchanceté et la générosité, c'est ça la vérité. Savoir qu'il n'y a pas que la générosité ou que la méchanceté mais une sorte de tango.

8. Blaise Cendrars, illustration for Christophe Gallaz, Etienne Delessert *Suisse flamboyante. Trente portraits de créateurs*, watercolour, Zoé and Gallimard, 1997

a metaphor for my moving between continents. I wrote and drew it all by myself. It would take too long to recount the whole of this emigration story, which is both readily understandable for children aged four to eight and full of subtext that appeals to adults. Jean-Claude Carrière and I worked on a script to turn it into a feature-length film.

JP: Our interview is drawing to an end, and yet we have missed out so many great names…

ED: …too many to list. I should at least mention Rita Marshall, my wife of 40 years, an outstanding typographer – an artistic director, in fact, working with artists and writers from the first line or the first sketch. Looking back on her achievements over 30 years with Creative Editions, it's clear that she's a fully fledged designer in the sense that she made the work of many creators shine. There's something of her in every single one of those books. We have worked side by side and even collaborated on a number of books. She wrote two: *I Hate To Read* and *I Still Hate To Read*.

JP: One last word, perhaps?

ED: We must see the good and the bad in everything around us, the malice and the generosity, that's the truth. We must remember that life isn't all benevolent or all malevolent, it's a sort of tango between the two.

K, L, M, N

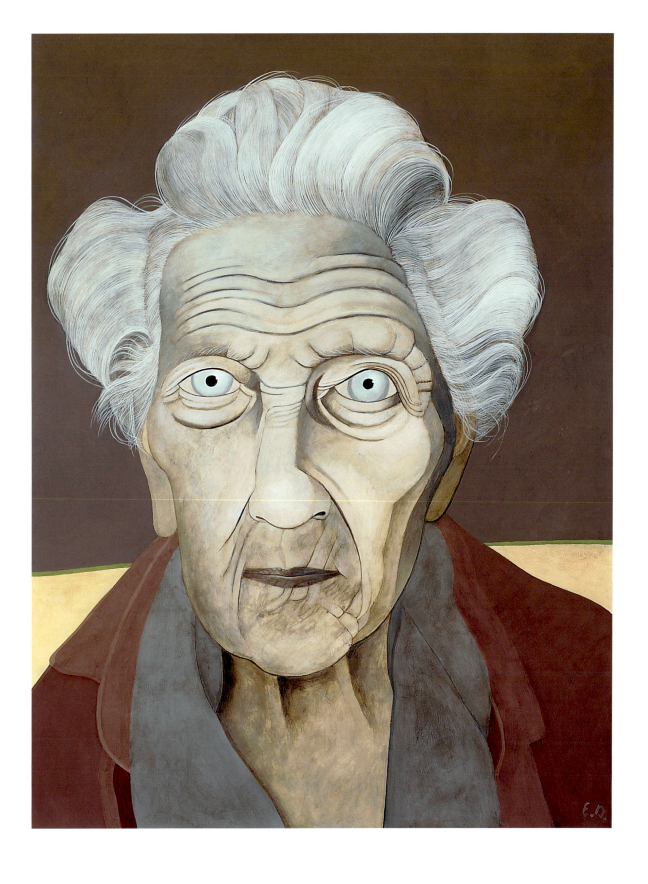

P, Q

9
neuf poires

T, U

Etienne Delessert
Scrivo disegni, dipingo idee

di Jacques Poget

Ricorrendo a questa formula intrigante, Etienne Delessert non vuole giocare con un paradosso, ma definire esattamente il suo particolare talento. Di solito, scrivere e disegnare sono due attività nettamente separate, anche se praticate dallo stesso autore: basti pensare a Jean Dubuffet (il cui talento letterario merita grande attenzione, come d'altronde quello di Etienne Delessert). Uno scrittore, salvo quando è esclusivamente un poeta, si rivolge in larga misura all'intelletto, mentre un artista visivo, salvo quando è un disegnatore tecnico, fa ampio appello alle emozioni.

Etienne Delessert coniuga invece le due modalità per «harmoniser l'environnement humain» (armonizzare l'ambiente umano); questa è infatti la funzione del design secondo il dizionario francese Larousse, mentre il tedesco Duden parla di «formgerechte und funktionale Gestaltgebung» (progettare in modo funzionale e adeguato alla forma). Entrambe le definizioni si attagliano alle opere di Etienne Delessert, sia ai libri e film per bambini e alle illustrazioni su riviste, sia ai manifesti, che lo hanno reso uno dei «Maîtres de l'imaginaire» (Maestri dell'immaginario, nome della fondazione da lui stesso creata per tramandare le opere dei suoi coevi).

L'immaginazione, il «trasformare la realtà», pervade tutta la vita di Etienne Delessert.

Che scriva E disegni l'allegoria del suo destino, o la metafora di quest'ultimo, in *La Corne de Brume* (Il corno da nebbia), oppure che crei in lungometraggio una versione personalissima de *Il flauto magico*, o ancora che attinga alle fonti dell'artista Saul Steinberg, dello psicologo e logico Jean Piaget o del poeta Maurice Chappaz, il suo unico scopo è aprire l'accesso a una dimensione superiore, a una più ampia libertà di pensiero e di emozioni. Quando reclamizza e vende l'acqua di Evian o illustra per il New York Times la tragedia della navicella spaziale Columbia, quando crea le animazioni di Yok-Yok o spinge un topo all'esplorazione di un mondo sconosciuto, Etienne Delessert riesce ogni volta a inventare la forma più adeguata e più funzionale per abbinare concezione ed emozione estetica. Ai suoi occhi, il prodotto commerciale e l'approccio intellettuale, il racconto per bambini e i ritratti di personaggi straordinari non rispondono a una gerarchia di valori: tutte le sue creazioni richiedono un'attenzione ugualmente intensa, un'identica audacia.

Il ricco tracciato dei suoi 60 anni di carriera è stupefacente. Con la maturità classica in tasca, sceglie di non intraprendere il percorso universitario, decide di trasmettere visivamente le sue idee, lavora in un'agenzia grafica e si approccia al disegno da autodidatta, ispirandosi alla rivista *Graphis* e ai manifesti degli anni Sessanta, dominati da figure svizzero-tedesche di spicco quali Herbert Leupin, Celestino Piatti e Armin Hofmann. La sua sensibilità per l'arte che si incontra per strada e sui giornali fa di lui l'erede, pur molto indiretto, di questi grandi precursori.

Per due volte abbandona una posizione ormai consolidata per il desiderio di imparare qualcosa di diverso: prima a Parigi, dove conquista il colore, inizialmente per i suoi manifesti pubblicitari, poi a New York, città di Milton Glaser e della brigata del Push Pin Studio. Ne trae ispirazione in profondità: il suo stile non imita nessuno, anche se è ricco di allusioni, da Jérôme Bosch (secondo Eugène Ionesco) al suo amico André François. Etienne Delessert non rinnega queste influenze e accoglie sia i più anziani, che i coetanei, che i più giovani, con la generosità che l'ha condotto a creare i Maestri dell'immaginario per l'illustrazione e il sito *ricochet.org* per il disegno per bambini, o a organizzare un'esposizione omaggio per Heinz Edelmann.

Ma Delessert diviene Delessert ascoltando... sé stesso. La critica Françoise Jaunin non lo ricollega «a nessun movimento, salvo che per il versante pittorico, il lato oscuro della sua opera: la vena espressiva e grottesca, l'espressionismo ampio e atemporale di tutti gli artisti che traducono la loro angoscia esistenziale nella veemenza del gesto e nel rilascio impulsivo delle emozioni. A questo, Etienne Delessert aggiunge tutta la parte di oscurità fantasmagorica che si può ritrovare in particolare in James Ensor».

Siamo lontani da una scuola di pensiero, è lui che fa scuola, nello stesso modo indiretto, nell'ambito specifico dei libri (e poi dei film) per bambini. Dopo Maurice Sendak e Tomi Ungerer, colleghi rispettati e ammirati, Etienne Delessert apre una via originale. E forse è il suo modo di pensare che rinnova tale ambito, ancor più della sua espressione grafica, anche se quest'ultima impressiona, soprattutto i giovani artisti che lavorano con lui presso lo studio Carabosse o alla casa editrice Tournesol. Monique Félix, John Howe e tanti altri ci sono passati e ne conservano una certa memoria, ma senza imitarlo.

Caso raro, questo artista che lavora da solo è stato quindi per anni un caposquadra e un imprenditore, ha animato laboratori, lanciato case editrici e società di produzione con decine di titoli all'attivo, e addirittura pubblicato lavori dei suoi allievi. «Etienne Delessert ha dato a tutta una generazione l'idea e la certezza che il libro per bambini è un genere artistico e letterario a pieno titolo, letteratura ricca di nobilità», sottolinea l'esperta Janine Kotwica.

Delessert pensa «bambino»

Sin dal suo arrivo a Parigi, dove si guadagna da vivere con campagne pubblicitarie innovative, Etienne Delessert inizia a pensare ai bambini e a lavorare per loro. Un giorno si rende conto che, come tutti gli autori, crea pensando di ricordare il bambino che lui stesso è stato, ma in realtà non conosce davvero il modo di pensare del suo pubblico. C'è un uomo che conosce bene l'argomento, a Ginevra: Jean Piaget, professore di psicologia sperimentale e filosofo. Il vodese di New York lo va a trovare, gli fa domande, lo conquista, lavora sotto la sua supervisione con l'assistente, Odile Mosimann. Quest'ultima svolge presso dozzine di bambini un'indagine su misura, finalizzata a comprendere come reagiscono alle storie inventate e disegnate dagli adulti e come elaborano e disegnano le loro storie. L'album chiave *Comment la souris reçoit une pierre sur la tête et découvre le monde* nasce direttamente dai risultati di questa ricerca ma anche, cosa essenziale, dalla capacità di ascolto e di apertura dei ricercatori. In questo contesto, la prefazione di Jean Piaget è un caso rarissimo di competenza e umiltà scientifica al servizio di un approccio artistico.

Artistico e spirituale, perché molte immagini dell'agnostico Etienne Delessert sono pervase dalla verticalità della trascendenza. La natura stessa, minerale e vegetale, condivide con le sue creature (animali, uomini, mostri e angeli) due qualità singolari: l'imprevedibilità e il misterioso potere dello sguardo. Quando le osserviamo, ci sentiamo a nostra volta scrutati da loro, ne percepiamo la potenza.

Nelle opere di Etienne Delessert si avverte ovunque il respiro della libertà e dell'immaginazione. Lo ha capito molto presto Eugène Ionesco, che ha scritto «Delessert scopre la bellezza, una sorta di grandioso affresco di esseri e oggetti che si dispiega nel colore e attraverso il colore».

Jacques Poget, giornalista e cronista, ha lavorato per la stampa quotidiana e periodica, per la televisione e per la radio, è stato corrispondente dagli Stati Uniti, caporedattore de L'Illustré e di 24Heures e presidente del Circolo letterario di Losanna. Si è specializzato in ritrattistica e nella conduzione di incontri letterari.

Etienne Delessert

I write pictures, and I paint ideas

by Jacques Poget

The somewhat pithy quote from Etienne Delessert above is not intended to be paradoxical but rather a precise definition of his particular talent. Writing and drawing are usually so neatly separated from each other, even when produced by the same person. Dubuffet's writings, for example, warrant close attention, as do Delessert's. Writers of anything but pure poetry are chiefly concerned with intellect. Visual artists, with the exception of technical draughtspeople, are chiefly concerned with emotions.

What Delessert does is marry the two disciplines in a way that satisfies the definition of design according to both the French Larousse ("harmonising the human environment") and the German Duden ("reconciling form and function"). This is reflected in his books and films for children, his illustrations for magazines and his posters, which have earned him a place among the "Maîtres de l'Imaginaire" ("Masters of the Imaginary", the name of the foundation he set up to preserve his peers' works).

Imagination has been a central theme throughout Delessert's life as he has sought to "transform reality".

Whether writing and drawing the allegory or metaphor of his destiny in *Ashes, Ashes*, dreaming up a highly personal feature-length *Magic Flute* or drawing inspiration from the artist Saul Steinberg, the psychologist and logician Jean Piaget or the poet Maurice Chappaz, his sole aim is to transport us to a higher plane with greater freedom of thought and emotion. Whether advertising Evian mineral water, illustrating the disaster that befell the space shuttle Columbia for the *New York Times*, filming Yok-Yok or sending a mouse out into a world of discovery, he navigates ideas and emotions to come up with "the most fitting and most functional form". Commercial product or intellectual exercise, children's tale or portrait of an exceptional person – he does not see any as more valuable than the rest, and all his creations receive the same meticulous, bold attention.

The rich variety of a career spanning sixty years is astonishing. After focussing on the Classics in his school leaver's exams, Delessert eschewed university in favour of a career in visual communication. He found a job at a graphic design agency and became a self-taught illustrator. His influences included *Graphis* magazine and 1960s poster art, which was dominated by such greats of German-speaking Switzerland as Herbert Leupin, Celestino Piatti and Armin Hofmann. This affinity for art that can be seen on the street and in the newspapers made him – very indirectly – a successor to those great pioneers.

He quit two jobs to venture further afield and keep learning. In Paris, he mastered colour, initially for advertising posters. Then he moved on to New York, home of Milton Glaser and his Push Pin Studios colleagues. Delessert absorbed a wide a range of influences. His style alludes to many, from Hieronymus Bosch (according to Eugène Ionesco) to his friend André François, but never imitates. He acknowledges his influences and respects his elders, contemporaries and the younger generation with a generosity that has given us the "Les Maîtres de l'Imaginaire" foundation for illustration, the website ricochet.org for children's design and an exhibition in honour of Heinz Edelmann.

However, Delessert found his niche by listening to…himself. For the critic Françoise Jaunin, he cannot be ascribed "to any movement, although his paintings reveal the dark side of his work: an expressive and grotesque vein, the broad, timeless expressionism of all artists who convey their existential angst through bold gestures and the impulsive release of emotions. Delessert adds that whole phantasmagorical darkness that we find, in particular, in James Ensor's work."

Far removed from any school, Delessert himself took on the role of teacher, again indirectly, in his books and films for children. Following Sendak and Ungerer, colleagues he respected and admired, he blazed his own trail. It was perhaps his way of thinking that breathed new life into the genre even more than his visual expression. Of course, that expression left an impression on the young artists who worked with him at the Carabosse studio and the publishing firm Tournesol. Monique Félix, John Howe and many others passed through there and kept something of the spirit without ever imitating Delessert.

He is a rare example of the solitary artist who has, over the years, also led teams, been an entrepreneur, overseen workshops, launched publishing and production firms with dozens of titles to their name and published works by his own protégés. "He has given a whole generation the notion and the assurance that children's books constitute a worthy artistic and literary genre in their own right," stresses the expert Janine Kotwica.

Delessert seeks to think like a child

From the moment he arrived in Paris, where he made a living from innovative advertising, Delessert started to think about producing works aimed at children. One day, he realised that, like all authors, he believed that he was writing from the memory of the child he once was without really understanding how his audience thinks. One man who knew a lot about this subject was Jean Piaget, professor of experimental psychology and philosophy in Geneva. Delessert travelled from New York to Geneva to interview him, and the professor was so responsive to his queries that he assigned his assistant, Odile Mosimann, to launch a research project addressing the artist's concerns. Involving several dozen children, the study aimed to understand how children respond to stories written and illustrated by adults and how they write and illustrate their own stories. The picture book *How the mouse was hit on the head by a stone and so discovered the world*, a metaphor for the shock of birth, was a direct result of the findings of this research. Most importantly, the book was made possible by the researchers' openness and ability to listen. The foreword by Piaget is an extremely rare example of scientific expertise and humility in the service of artistic endeavour.

Artistry with a spiritual trait; the agnostic Delessert frequently hints to the vertical axis of transcendency which structures many of his pictorial works. Even the natural world, both mineral and vegetable, shares two things in common with his creatures, be they animal, human, monster or angel: unpredictability and the mysterious power of the gaze – when we look at them, we get a strong feeling that they are looking back at us.

A sense of freedom and imagination pervades his works. Eugène Ionesco recognised it very early on, writing that "…Delessert discovers beauty, a sort of grandiose evolution of beings and objects in colour and through colour."

Jacques Poget is a journalist and columnist who has worked in daily newspapers, magazines, television and radio, as a correspondent in the US, Editor-in-Chief of L'Illustré and 24Heures and President of the Lausanne Literary Circle. He specialises in profile stories and hosting literary events.

[DE → p. 9, FR → p. 10]

Biography

Born in Lausanne on 4 January 1941
Lives and works in Lakeville, Connecticut

1951–59 Classical studies in Latin and Greek.
1959 Works at Art Studio Maffei in Pully.
1962 Graphic design for Cahiers de la Renaissance vaudoise (CRV) and illustrations for *Kafka contre l'absurde* by Joël Jakubec (CRV).
1963 Moves to Paris. Works with Studio Hollenstein; freelance work in advertising (Publicis for Shell and Golf de Valcros). First drawings in colour.
1964 Artistic direction for *Formidable* and *Twenty* magazines.
1965 Moves to New York. Drawings for magazines (*Mc Call's, Redbook, Fact, Family Circle*). Advertising work for Time-Life Books. Book covers.
1967 *Graphis* magazine (no. 128) features him in an article and on the cover.
The Endless Party (Harlin Quist), first book illustrated by Delessert. Multiple joint editions – and multiple counterfeits.
1968 Illustrates *Story Number 1 by Ionesco* (Harlin Quist). *Story Number 2 by Ionesco* is published in 1970, *Stories 1,2,3,4* in 2009 by Gallimard.
Illustrates *Le match Valais-Judée* by Maurice Chappaz.
1971 *How the mouse was hit on the head by a stone and so discovered the world.* (Good Book-Doubleday); *"…an astonishing blend of euphoria, joie de vivre, non-conformism and incisive observation accompanied by constant humour."* – Jean Piaget.
The book is turned into a play by Théâtre Am Stram Gram, with sets and costumes designed by Delessert. The play is performed hundreds of times in Switzerland and France. 13-minute animated film.
Sets up the publishing house Good Book in New York together with Herb Lubalin.
1973 On returning to Lausanne, founds Carabosse, a studio that produces animated films for television. Works on a dozen films with Sesame Street. The studio has a number of talented staff, including Monique Felix and John Howe.
1975 Retrospective at the Musée des Arts Décoratifs / Louvre, Paris, after Hockney and at the same time as Le Corbusier.

1977 Founds the publishing house Tournesol together with Anne van der Essen and creates *Yok-Yok*. 150 ten-second short films for SAP, then 12 books published jointly with Gallimard. Success throughout Europe as well as in Japan and Korea, unlicensed editions in Iran. Album *Yok-Yok chante*, with music by Henri Dès.
Tournesol-Carabosse goes on to publish over 50 titles, including the first illustrated works by a number of the studio's animators and three books about the environment (the first of their kind) starring the mouse. Album *La Souris s'en va-t-en Guerre*, with music by Andy Kulberg.
Produces a 30-minute pilot for French television and Bayard Presse of *Tic et Tac, Coq et Poule*, a series for young people.
1981 Begins production of the animated film *Supersaxo*, after the story by Chappaz, with a staff of almost 50. After a producer pulls out, the film is abandoned in 1984.
1983–84 Oversees the publication of *20 fairy tales*, featuring popular stories interpreted by great illustrators (Edelmann, Chwast, Topor, André François, Tardi, Innocenti etc.) as well as the photographers Sarah Moon and Marcel Imsand. The series (with artistic direction by Rita Marshall, published by Creative Editions, Grasset-Monsieur Chat and Tournesol) has come to be seen as a milestone in the history of publishing.
1985 Takes up residence in the US. Divides his time between books, painting and editorial work for the *New York Times*, *The Atlantic* and *Le Monde*.
1990 Publishes *Ashes, Ashes* (Stewart Tabori & Chang).
1991 Retrospectives at the Palazzo delle Esposizioni in Rome and the Museum of Decorative Arts in Lausanne.
Monograph *Etienne Delessert* (Gallimard, in New York Stewart, Tabori and Chang).
1992 *Prophets and Pretenders*, 100 imaginary portraits, exhibited at the Musée Jenisch in Vevey.
1993–94 Retrospectives at the Library of Congress, Washington, and in eight major US cities.
1997 *Suisse flamboyante*, portraits of famous Swiss people, exhibition and book (Zoé and Gallimard).
1998 Retrospective at the Olympic Museum in Lausanne.

1999	Retrospective at the School of Visual Arts in New York. Jean-Claude Carrière writes foreword to *Etienne Delessert* (Poche Illustrateur, Delpire). *"A child is more than a child. Often, even more than an adult."* – Jean-Claude Carrière.	2015	Illustrations for *Ubu Roi* (Gallimard). Organises a Heinz Edelman retrospective at Espace Arlaud in Lausanne.
2001	*Les Affiches d'Etienne Delessert*, published by Cramer and Gallimard	2016	Exhibition catalogue for *Rita Marshall, Lion Tamer* (École Estienne, Paris)
2008–09	Provides *Siné Hebdo* with 86 weekly cartoons on US politics.	2017	Sets up the Swiss foundation Les Maîtres de l'Imaginaire. Exhibition *Sbalzi d'umor*, Galleria Nuages, Milan.
2009	Retrospective *Pourquoi grandir?*, Youth Illustration Museum, Moulins.	2019	Retrospective at the Tsinghua Art Museum in Beijing.
2010	Exhibition *Suite américaine*, Château de Saint-Maurice.	1994–2008	Exhibitions of drawings and paintings on the themes of *Petites Lumières du Paradis, Birds of Prey, The Cat Collection, Suisse flamboyante, Un Oeil noir te regarde, des Anges, Stories of the Lake (Wononscopomuc), Le Feu* and *Mélodies*.
2011	Exhibition *Mélodies* (song lyrics from Bob Dylan and Ray Charles to Stravinsky/Ramuz). New series of *Yok-Yok* albums. The originals are exhibited at the Salon du Livre in Geneva. *What a circus!*, retrospective at the Eric Carle Museum in Amherst, Massachusetts.	2007–22	20 illustrated books. European Award, 1976; Premio Grafico Fiera di Bologna per l'Infanzia, 1981 and 1989; Biennial of Illustration Bratislava gold plaque, 1969, 1979 and 1985. In total, 13 gold and 12 silver medals from the Society of Illustrators in New York.
2013	*A Glass* (Creative Editions), portrait of his mother Eglantine. Retrospective *Étienne Delessert: Plein Cadre*, École Estienne, Paris.		

Gran Premio svizzero di design 2023

In un'epoca in cui la globalizzazione sembra toccare tutti gli aspetti della nostra vita, è legittimo interrogarsi sulla pertinenza di un premio rivolto unicamente a creatrici e creatori svizzeri. Al giorno d'oggi ha ancora senso celebrare il meglio del design ponendo un limite come il colore del passaporto? Esiste in Svizzera una tradizione sufficientemente solida da motivare, nel 2023, un Gran Premio di design? Indubbiamente, per anni le scuole di arte applicata hanno formato designer, grafici e fotografi che, a loro volta, hanno forgiato la reputazione del nostro Paese all'estero. Max Bill, Adrian Frutiger, Jean Widmer, Fritz Haller, Armin Hofmann o Robert Frank compaiono in tutte le enciclopedie del mondo. E Helvetica è il nome di un carattere tipografico entrato in un museo e noto anche ai non professionisti del settore. È innegabile che, nel Novecento, molti tra i creatori usciti dalla celebre Kunstgewerbeschule di Zurigo hanno contribuito all'eccellente reputazione del design svizzero. Si potrebbe persino parlare di una grafica svizzera come si parla di un'alta moda francese o di un cinema italiano. Ma qual è la situazione oggi? Esiste davvero un design svizzero?

Il design che qui celebriamo è presente ovunque nelle nostre vite. Si riferisce agli oggetti, ai vestiti, ai testi e alle immagini che ci circondano. Può avere la forma di una sedia, una scarpa, un poster, un libro, un videogioco, un sito web, una scenografia o un lavoro fotografico. Oggi, la nuova generazione che si dedica a ricercare nel campo del design adotta progressivamente approcci interdisciplinari e metodologie ibride, intreccia analogico e digitale, mescola materiali e tradizioni, ricicla e innova, si appropria, crea e trasforma, passando dal naturale all'artificiale. I confini si confondono. Il Gran Premio svizzero di design celebra artisti che hanno avuto carriere particolarmente interessanti, rende omaggio a professionisti che hanno segnato la storia della loro disciplina e permette di assegnare una distinzione a persone che finora non hanno ricevuto il dovuto riconoscimento. Da oltre un secolo, premi e medaglie fanno entrare nella storia vari artisti, di qualsiasi ambito. A lungo questi riconoscimenti erano riservati agli uomini. Nel 2023, come in passato, i premi offrono agli artisti il riconoscimento dei loro pari. Tuttavia, il pantheon dei grandi uomini non può continuare a ignorare le donne che da tempo contribuiscono allo sviluppo della loro disciplina. Oggi più che mai, è nostro dovere includere anche i nomi delle creatrici lasciate nell'ombra. Parimenti, considerata la ricchezza e diversità regionale, culturale e linguistica della Svizzera, è necessario che questa distinzione federale venga decentralizzata e valorizzi anche personalità che operano al di fuori dei classici centri urbani.

Cosa ci rivela dunque il Gran Premio svizzero di design 2023? Con il riconoscimento di Etienne Delessert, Eleonore Peduzzi Riva e Chantal Prod'Hom, la commissione ha voluto dimostrare che il campo del design è esteso, che tocca tutte le generazioni, anche i bambini, che è una materia da vedere, toccare, pensare e sognare e che la creazione «svizzera» oltrepassa spesso le frontiere del nostro Paese. Infine, il Gran Premio 2023 proclama altresì la necessità di rivedere la storia del design attraverso la lente del genere e di far cadere le gerarchie tra le varie discipline.

Nathalie Herschdorfer, presidente della Commissione federale del design

Introduzione

Il Gran Premio svizzero di design è il massimo riconoscimento del nostro Paese per questo settore della produzione artistica. Dal 2007 l'Ufficio federale della cultura lo assegna ogni anno a tre designer o studi di design svizzeri che hanno contribuito in modo determinante a dare lustro al design svizzero a livello nazionale e internazionale. Il premio promuove, rafforza e valorizza la scena del design e le sue tradizioni. Quest'anno i Gran Premi svizzeri di design rendono omaggio all'illustratore Etienne Delessert, alla designer Eleonore Peduzzi Riva e alla storica dell'arte Chantal Prod'Hom.

Nel preparare la presente pubblicazione ci siamo resi conto, ancora una volta, che scegliere una sola qualifica professionale fra le molte discipline attinenti al design risulta troppo riduttivo per riassumere i numerosi campi di attività delle persone interessate. Ciò vale anche per i tre protagonisti di quest'anno, le cui competenze e risorse sono il frutto di carriere multidisciplinari e per nulla lineari.

Etienne Delessert, ad esempio, è un *illustratore* di libri per bambini, ma non solo. Inizia la sua carriera come grafico e diventa famoso per le sue campagne pubblicitarie e i manifesti. Lavora poi come *illustratore per la stampa*, tra l'altro per il New «York Times» e «The Atlantic». È anche imprenditore e nella sua carriera fonda due case editrici e uno studio di animazione. Forse è meglio conosciuto per essere l'*inventore* di Yok-Yok, tanto amato durante la nostra infanzia.

Eleonore Peduzzi Riva, di formazione architetto d'interni, ha esercitato questa attività durante l'epoca d'oro del design italiano. Come *designer industriale*, crea mobili per marchi famosi come de Sede o Zanotta. Come *designer di prodotto*, realizza un posacenere iconico per Artemide. A Milano è conosciuta principalmente per il suo ruolo di *consulente di marca* per numerose aziende.

Dopo gli studi della storia dell'arte Chantal Prod'Hom lavora come *curatrice* d'arte contemporanea. Molto presto apre il suo primo museo, la Fondation Asher Edelman a Pully, di cui può definirsi *co-direttrice*. È però nella sua funzione di *direttrice esecutiva* del centro Fabrica di Treviso che entra per la prima volta in contatto con la scena del design. Successivamente inaugura il mudac, Musée de design et d'arts appliqués contemporains, dove lavora come *direttrice del museo* fino al 2022. In questa veste influenza quale *mediatrice* il dibattito nazionale sul design e partecipa a numerose giurie e commissioni come *ambasciatrice* del design svizzero.

Per l'Ufficio federale della cultura questo premio rappresenta ogni anno un'opportunità per rafforzare la consapevolezza nei confronti del design svizzero e della sua importanza per l'identità culturale del nostro Paese. Un premio alla carriera è anche uno stimolo per la prossima generazione di designer a impegnarsi con passione per le proprie idee. Per i vincitori e le vincitrici questo riconoscimento ufficiale da parte del proprio Paese nonché della comunità costituisce un traguardo importante: ora fanno formalmente parte della storia del design svizzero.

I vincitori e le vincitrici vengono proposti da una giuria di esperti, la Commissione federale del design, che ringrazio per aver selezionato personalità eccezionali: queste sono la migliore dimostrazione di come il design arricchisce le nostre vite.

Anna Niederhäuser
Responsabile Premi svizzeri di design
Ufficio federale della cultura

Swiss Grand Award for Design 2023

In an age when globalisation affects every aspect of our lives, one might well question the relevance of an award that exclusively recognises Swiss creators. Can we still celebrate the best in design while imposing a restriction based on what passport a person holds? Does Switzerland really have a strong enough tradition to justify a Grand Award for Design in 2023? It is true to say that, for a long time, our universities of applied arts produced designers, draughtspeople and photographers who forged an international reputation for Switzerland. Max Bill, Adrian Frutiger, Jean Widmer, Fritz Haller, Armin Hofmann and Robert Frank, for example, are all recognised as leading lights. Indeed, a typeface bearing the name Helvetica has become so archetypal that it is well known among non-designers. There is no denying that a number of creators emerged in the 20th century, especially from Zurich's famous Kunstgewerbeschule, who were instrumental in raising the profile of Swiss design. We can even speak of Swiss graphic design in the same way that we do of French *haute couture* or Italian cinema. But can we really say that there is such a thing as "Swiss design" today?

The design we are celebrating here permeates our lives in the form of objects, clothing, visuals, text and images that surround us. It could be a chair, a shoe, a poster, a book, a videogame, a website, a set or a photograph. The up-and-coming designers of today's younger generation are increasingly adopting interdisciplinary approaches and hybrid methods that combine analogue and digital, materials and traditions. They recycle, innovate, appropriate, create and transform, shifting between the natural and the artificial. Lines are becoming blurred. The Swiss Grand Award for Design honours artists who have had particularly interesting careers, pays homage to professionals who have made history in their field and recognises individuals who have not yet received the appreciation they deserve. For more than a century, awards and medals have secured a place in the history books for artists in all domains. They were an exclusively male preserve for a long time. In 2023, as in the past, awards offer artists the recognition of their peers. Now more than ever, it is our duty to bring female creators out of the shadows and into the limelight. Since Switzerland boasts such diversity in terms of regions, cultures and languages, it is also vital for this federal award to broaden its scope and honour those who work outside the main cities.

What, then, can we learn from the Swiss Grand Award for Design 2023? In choosing Etienne Delessert, Eleonore Peduzzi Riva and Chantal Prod'Hom, the Commission wished to show what a broad field design is; how it affects all generations, children included; that it is something visible, tangible, thought-provoking and dream-inspiring; and that "Swiss creation" often transcends national borders. Ultimately, this year's Grand Award also shows us

how essential it is to review the history of design from a gender perspective and break down the perceived hierarchy of professions.
Nathalie Herschdorfer, Chair of the Federal Design Commission

Introduction

The Swiss Grand Award for Design is our country's highest honour in this field and has been presented by the Federal Office of Culture every year since 2007 to three designers or design studios that have made a major contribution to the reputation of Swiss design on a national or international level. It is intended to promote, support and celebrate the design scene and its traditions. This year's recipients are the illustrator Etienne Delessert, the designer Eleonore Peduzzi Riva and the art historian Chantal Prod'Hom.

While compiling this publication, we were once again reminded that a single label cannot suffice to describe the wide variety of different professions that make up the field. This has never been more true than this year, with three recipients whose skills and experience are the product of interdisciplinary rather than linear design careers.

Etienne Delessert, for instance, is an *illustrator* of children's books, but he began his career as a *graphic designer*, making a name for himself through advertising campaigns and posters. As a *press illustrator*, meanwhile, he has worked for "The New York Times" and "The Atlantic". He is also an *entrepreneur*, having founded two publishing houses and a film studio. Delessert is perhaps best known as the *inventor* of a beloved character from our childhoods, Yok-Yok.

Eleonore Peduzzi Riva, for her part, trained as an *interior architect*, a profession she practised during the golden age of Italian design. As an *industrial designer*, she developed furniture for such leading brands as de Sede and Zanotta. As a *product designer*, she created an iconic ashtray for Artemide. In Milan, she is known primarily as a *brand consultant* to various companies.

Chantal Prod'Hom worked as a *curator* for contemporary art after graduating from university in art history. It was not long before she opened her first museum, the Asher Edelmann Foundation in Pully, and took on the role of *Co-Director*. Her first contact with design came when she was *Executive Director* of the Fabrica workshop in Treviso. She later launched the mudac, Museum of Contemporary Design and Applied Arts, staying on as its *Director* until the end of 2022. She influenced Swiss discourse on design in this role as a *mediator* and continues to serve as an *ambassador* for Swiss design through her membership of numerous juries and committees.

The Federal Office of Culture sees this award as an annual opportunity to raise the profile of Swiss design and highlight its importance for our country's cultural identity. A lifetime achievement award inspires the next generation of designers to strive for excellence in their own work. For the recipients, this official recognition from their homeland and peers is a true seal of approval that cements their place in Swiss design history.

They were nominated by a jury of experts, the Federal Design Commission. I would like to thank the members of the Commission for their excellent choices, which are the best possible proof of how design enriches our lives.

Anna Niederhäuser
Head of Design
Federal Office of Culture

[DE → p. 3, FR → p. 5]

Swiss Grand Award for Design Winners 2007–23

2023
Etienne Delessert
 Illustrator and
 graphic designer
Eleonore Peduzzi Riva
 Interior architect
 and consultant
Chantal Prod'Hom
 Museum director and curator

2022
Susanne Bartsch
 Talent curator
 and event producer
Verena Huber
 Interior architect
Beat Streuli
 Artist

2021
Julia Born
 Graphic designer
Peter Knapp
 Photographer and art director
Sarah Owens
 Design educator
 and researcher

2020
Ida Gut
 Fashion designer
Monique Jacot
 Photographer
Kueng Caputo
 Product designers

2019
Rosmarie Baltensweiler
 Product designer
Connie Hüsser
 Interior stylist
Thomi Wolfensberger
 Lithographer and publisher

2018
Cécile Feilchenfeldt
 Textile designer
Felco
 Product design
Rosmarie Tissi
 Graphic designer

2017
David Bielander
 Jewellery designer
Thomas Ott
 Illustrator
Jean Widmer
 Graphic designer
 and art director

2016
Claudia Caviezel
 Textile designer
Hans Eichenberger
 Product and interior designer
Ralph Schraivogel
 Graphic designer

2015
Luc Chessex
 Photographer
Lora Lamm
 Graphic designer
Team '77
 Typographers and
 type designers

2014
Erich Biehle
 Textile designer
Alfredo Häberli
 Furniture and product
 designer
Wolfgang Weingart
 Typographer

2013
Trix & Robert Haussmann
 Interior and product
 designers
Armin Hofmann
 Graphic designer
Martin Leuthold
 Textile designer

2012
Franco Clivio
 Product designer
Gavillet & Rust
 Graphic designers
Karl Gerstner
 Graphic designer

2011
Jörg Boner
 Product designer
NORM
 Graphic designers
Ernst Scheidegger
 Photographer
Walter Steiger
 Footwear designer

2010
Susi & Ueli Berger
 Furniture designers
Jean-Luc Godard
 Filmmaker
Sonnhild Kestler
 Textile designer
Otto Künzli
 Jewellery designer

2009
Robert Frank
 Photographer
Christoph Hefti
 Textile designer
Ursula Rodel
 Fashion designer
Thut Möbel
 Furniture design

2008
Holzer Kobler Architekturen
 Exhibition designers and
 architects
Albert Kriemler (Akris)
 Fashion designer
Alain Kupper
 Graphic designer, musician,
 artist
Walter Pfeiffer
 Photographer

2007
Ruth Grüninger
 Fashion designer
NOSE Communication
 design, service design
Bernhard Schobinger
 Jewellery designer
Cornel Windlin
 Graphic designer

Swiss Federal Design Commission 2023

Chair
Nathalie Herschdorfer
 Director, Photo Elysée

Members
Cécile Feilchenfeldt,
 Textile designer, Paris
Davide Fornari
 Professor for Research
 and Development at ECAL,
 Renens
David Glättli
 Industrial designer and
 creative director, Zurich/
 Tokyo
Andreas Gysin
 Programmer and graphic
 designer, Lugano
Vera Sacchetti
 Design critic and curator,
 Basel
Ivan Sterzinger
 Graphic designer and
 publisher, Zurich

The winners of the 2023 Swiss Grand Award for Design were selected by the 2022 commission.

Swiss Federal Design Commission 2022

Chair
Jörg Boner
 Product designer, Zurich

Members
Marietta Eugster
 Graphic designer, Paris
Cécile Feilchenfeldt,
 Textile designer, Paris
Davide Fornari
 Professor for Research
 and Development at ECAL,
 Renens
Nathalie Herschdorfer
 Director, Photo Elysée,
 Lausanne
Aude Lehmann
 Graphic designer, Zurich
Vera Sacchetti
 Design critic and curator,
 Basel

Colophon

Published on the occasion of the Swiss Grand Award for Design 2023

Head of project
 Anna Niederhäuser Federal
 Office of Culture (FOC), Bern

Editing, project coordination
 Mirjam Fischer, mille pages,
 Zurich

Art direction and design
 Ard – Guillaume Chuard
 Lausanne/London

Typeface
 LL Geigy, Robert Huber,
 Zurich

Photography (p. 7)
 © FOC / Diana Pfammatter
 (Eleonore Peduzzi Riva,
 Chantal Prod'Hom)
 © Robert F. Halko
 (Etienne Delessert)

Translations
 Paolo Giannoni (FR → IT),
 John Knox (IT → EN),
 Philippe Moser (FR/IT → DE),
 Mark O'Neil (FR → EN),
 Rodney Stringer (IT → EN),
 Marisa Sulmoni (DE/FR → IT),
 Aude Thalmann (DE → FR),
 Silvia Trevisan (FR → IT),
 Christian Viredaz (IT → FR),
 Myriam Walter (FR → DE)

Proofreading
 FOC Translation Services
 (DE / FR / IT)
 Mark O'Neil (EN)

Printing Gremper AG, Basel

Weitere Übersetzungen der
 Interviews finden Sie auf:
Veuillez trouver les traductions
 françaises sur :
La traduzione italiana delle
 interviste è disponibile su:
www.schweizerkulturpreise.ch/design

© 2023 the authors and Verlag Scheidegger & Spiess AG, Zurich

Texts © the authors
Images © the artists

Verlag Scheidegger & Spiess
Niederdorfstrasse 54
8001 Zürich, Switzerland
www.scheidegger-spiess.ch

Scheidegger & Spiess is being supported by the Federal Office of Culture with a general subsidy for the years 2021–24.

All rights reserved; no part of this publication may be reproduced, stored in a retrieval system or transmitted in any form or by any means, electronic, mechanical, photocopying, recording, or otherwise, without the prior written consent of the publisher.

The three winners of the Swiss Grand Award for Design 2023 are: Etienne Delessert, illustrator and graphic designer, Eleonore Peduzzi Riva, interior architect and consultant, and Chantal Prod'Hom, museum director and curator. The publication is distributed in a box containing three individual booklets – one for each winner.

ISBN: 978-3-03942-157-2

Schweizerische Eidgenossenschaft
Confédération suisse
Confederazione Svizzera
Confederaziun svizra

Eidgenössisches Departement des Innern EDI
Département fédéral de l'intérieur DFI
Dipartimento federale dell'interno DFI
Departament federal da l'intern DFI
Bundesamt für Kultur BAK
Office fédéral de la culture OFC
Ufficio federale della cultura UFC
Uffizi federal da cultura UFC